Praise for *Sacred Success*®

"With *Sacred Success*, you'll learn that not only can money and spirituality uplift each other; the health of our world depends on it. Barbara Stanny teaches women how to achieve financial freedom—with heart, soul, love, and a commitment to leaving the world better than we found it. What a blessing!"

—Lissa Rankin, MD, *New York Times* bestselling
author of *Mind Over Medicine*

"Financial success doesn't require giving up your dreams or personal values. In *Sacred Success*, Barbara Stanny shows that genuine success starts with staying true to yourself and embracing your passions. This is a fabulous read and an indispensable guide."

—Marci Shimoff, #1 *New York Times* bestselling author of *Happy for No Reason, Love for No Reason*, and *Chicken Soup for the Woman's Soul*

"*Sacred Success* is nothing less than inspired writing and reading. Only Barbara Stanny could write on the topic with this much insight and passion. If this book doesn't enable you to take a fresh look at your relationship with success, money, and wealth, nothing ever will."

—Lois P. Frankel, PhD, author of *Nice Girls Don't Get the Corner Office* and *Nice Girls Don't Get Rich*

"If you're ready to take charge of your finances and realize your full potential, this is your book. Barbara Stanny's expertise is, well, right on the money."

—Gabrielle Bernstein, *New York Times*
bestselling author of *Miracles Now*

"Barbara Stanny is a genius at articulating the steps a woman needs to take to step into a deeper level of power that has everything to do with higher service and nothing to do with power over. *Sacred Success* is a leading force in the paradigm shift the whole world is experiencing as we begin to embrace, celebrate, and benefit from the feminine. Read this book and be transformed."

—Kate Northrup, bestselling author of *Money: A Love Story*

"I've been recommending Barbara's books to my readers for years and thought I knew her story, but this dramatic retelling has so many arresting details she's never shared before—including how central her burgeoning spirituality was to her financial recovery. Her journey has been fascinating and her book is well worth reading for anyone who wants to make a life, rather than just a living."

—Liz Pulliam Weston, personal finance columnist
and author of *Deal with Your Debt*

"*Sacred Success* is absolutely phenomenal! I couldn't stop reading. It is a tour de force and EXACTLY what every woman needs to know. This book is a winner on so many levels. And it is written with passion, clarity, joy, and love."

—Christiane Northrup, MD, author of the *New York Times*
bestseller *Women's Bodies, Women's Wisdom*

"This groundbreaking book is about far more than money. It's a primer on creating wealth and wielding power as a woman."

—Marie Forleo, MarieForleo.com, founder of award-winning MarieTV

"*Sacred Success* is like hot yoga for your money beliefs. Barbara Stanny's revelations will have you bending your limitations, and reaching for deeper meaning—where the gold is."

—Danielle LaPorte, author of *The Desire Map* and *The Fire Starter Sessions*

"*Sacred Success* is for any woman who hungers for more. Not just to make more money, but to live a more meaningful life."

—Farnoosh Torabi, financial expert and author of *When
She Makes More: 10 Rules for Breadwinning Women*

"Ready to experience financial miracles? In *Sacred Success*, Barbara Stanny shows how taking control of your finances starts with honoring—and liberating—the authentic you. From that priceless well of self-rejuvenating power, Barbara guides you on the luminous path to achieving financial success on your own terms. A truly transformational read!"

—Manisha Thakor, CEO of MoneyZen Wealth Management

"It's time for women to redefine power and success on our own terms. Let Barbara show you the way!"

—Amanda Steinberg, founder of DailyWorth.com

SACRED SUCCESS®

SACRED SUCCESS®

A COURSE IN FINANCIAL MIRACLES

BARBARA STANNY

BenBella Books, Inc.

Dallas, TX

BenBella Books, Inc.
10300 N. Central Expressway
Suite #530
Dallas, TX 75231
www.benbellabooks.com
Send feedback to feedback@benbellabooks.com

Printed in the United States of America
10 9 8 7 6 5 4 3 2

Library of Congress Cataloging-in-Publication Data:

Stanny, Barbara.
   Sacred success : a course in financial miracles / Barbara Stanny.
      pages cm
   Includes bibliographical references and index.
   ISBN 978-1-940363-23-3 (hardback)—ISBN 978-1-940363-53-0 (electronic) 1.
Women—Finance, Personal. 2. Finance, Personal. 3. Success in business. I. Title.
   HG179.S796 2014
   332.0240082—dc23

                                                                    2014011136

Editing by Leah Wilson
Copyediting by Brittany Dowdle, Word Cat Editorial
Proofreading by Kristin Vorce and Rainbow Graphics
Cover design by Kit Sweeney and Rob Johnson
Jacket design by Kit Sweeney
Text design and composition by Publishers' Design and Production Services, Inc.
Printed by Lake Book Manufacturing

Distributed by Perseus Distribution
www.perseusdistribution.com
To place orders through Perseus Distribution:
Tel: (800) 343–4499
Fax: (800) 351–5073
Email: orderentry@perseusbooks.com

Significant discounts for bulk sales are available. Please contact Glenn Yeffeth at glenn@benbellabooks.com or (214) 750–3628.

*To my loving husband, Lee Huson,
and the wonderful memories of our
Suncadia writing retreats.*

"There can be no political revolution, no social revolution, no economic revolution. The only revolution is that of the spirit; it is individual. And if millions of individuals change, then society will change as a consequence, not vice versa. You cannot change the society first and hope that individuals will change later on."

—Osho
(with deep appreciation to Rha Goddess)

Contents

APPENDIX

Acknowledgments

"Gratitude goes hand in hand with love, and where one is the other must be found."

—A Course in Miracles

I want to acknowledge my sincere gratitude and say a heartfelt thank-you to:

Athena Burke, for the day I shared my dream of doing a seminar with gospel singing and you replied, "I sing gospel." Then you wrote "Jump." And *Sacred Success* slowly started taking shape. Every retreat is so much richer because of your soulful singing and your inspiring insights.

Lissa Rankin, for introducing me to my amazing agent. And to Michele Martin, for accepting me as client, expertly reshaping my proposal, and then, with the indispensable help of Steven and Gabriel Harris, finding the perfect publisher for this book.

Doris Ober, for bringing my earliest drafts to life, like a skilled doula, making sure they were presentable and ready to greet the world. This, our fourth go-around, was as delightful as always!

Jill Rogers, my closest confidante, for always being there, 24/7, whenever I needed your profound insights, unconditional love, overwhelming support, or sidesplitting giggles. Also to Richard Rogers for putting up with the countless times I called Jill to "spring-clean" my book (plus everything else!).

Donna Otmani, for your brilliant coaching and loving friendship as I struggled mightily with my resistance to writing this book.

Regina Thomashauer and Mama Gena's School of Womanly Arts, for introducing me to more power and joy than I could ever have anticipated, giving me a safe platform to test out my ideas, and providing a glorious community that has supported me and my work from the outset.

My spotter sisters (Suzy Carroll, Teresa Verraes, Kristin Manwaring, and Mary Deveneau), the most loving group of women I could ever imagine, for witnessing my struggles, rejoicing in my every win, reading my early drafts, and lovingly standing by my side through this whole process, from the "silver platter" to the finished product.

Suzy Carroll, my cherished friend, you deserve an extra shout-out for being the first person to listen as I described *Sacred Success* in detail during our walks, encouraging me to take it out into the world, signing up for my earliest teleclass and my very first retreat, returning again three times, using the teachings to incredibly transform your own life, then creating our spotters group. You've played a huge role in the birth of this work.

Leah Wilson, for your eagle eye, expert editing, and making it all so fun. You're a terrific editor, a pleasure to work with, and a total trooper through your first trimester.

Glenn Yeffeth and the staff at BenBella, for giving my book such a wonderful home and providing me with a delightfully unique and thoroughly enjoyable publishing experience.

Lee Huson, for loving, appreciating, and supporting me in a way no man ever has, just as you promised from the very beginning.

My beloved children (my daughters, Melissa, Julie, Anna; my sons [in-law], Siig and Jeff; and my grandbabies, Kaiden, Kaya, and Nakita), for the inspiration and joy you've consistently given me and for all the future babies I can't wait to meet.

The successful women who generously granted me an interview, giving me my first glimpse into this "new game" of wealth, and my

Sacred Success sisters who attended my retreats and taught me so much. Without all of you there would be no book.

Finally, my life, as this book, is deeply indebted to *A Course in Miracles*, a self-study guide for spiritual transformation. As you're about to read, the *Course* came to me exactly when I needed it, in the most random way—as is often the case for so many of its readers.

And So It Came to Be

"You do not ask too much of life but far too little."

—A Course in Miracles

When My World Fell Apart

One lovely spring day, in the sleepy suburb of Prairie Village, Kansas, as the robins were busily announcing their arrival, I lay curled up like a baby on the orange shag-carpeted floor of our bedroom, sobbing and shaking uncontrollably. I was a young housewife, in the early seventies, trapped in a terrible marriage with no one to turn to.

My husband, a compulsive gambler, was burning through our money—well, to be precise, *my* money, my inheritance—like a fire out of control. When I confronted him, he told me not to worry, swore he'd never do it again.

Those words, "Don't worry," were exactly what my dad used to say whenever I asked about finances growing up. My father (the R of H&R Block) genuinely didn't want me or any of his "girls" (my mom and two sisters) to ever worry. I trusted my father. I did the same with my husband. I insanely continued to believe his reassurances, even as things worsened. I had no other choice. I didn't understand finances, didn't know where my money was, how much I had, or even how to find out. He managed everything. My parents, who knew about my husband's gambling, were furious with me that I couldn't stop him. But I felt helpless.

Eventually, my husband stopped trying to reassure me. Instead, when confronted, he'd get defensive, talk in circles. And I'd walk away feeling like *I* was the one who'd done something wrong. Maybe if we had another baby, I thought, things would get better. Our precious daughter, Melissa, was almost six months old. But my body rebelled, and I was told I'd never have more children. Devastated, I fell deep into depression.

I thought I'd hit bottom, though that was still a long way off. My grief was unbearable. I had to do something. So I did what any crazed, codependent wife of an addict would do. I found an addiction of my own—work!

Betty Friedan's new book, *The Feminine Mystique*, had just come out. Women were reentering the work force in droves, hordes of eager housewives searching for more fulfilling lives. I was right there among them. Armed with a master's degree in counseling psychology, I found a job at the local university's women's center, helping these very women become employable.

I knew immediately that working with women was what I was meant to do. A few years later, I started my own company, The Career Management Center, which I believe was the first career counseling firm in Kansas City. I rented an office, hired a secretary, and found a graphic artist to design my logo. I passed out my cards like a Las Vegas dealer, and clients came, lots of them. Media began calling with interview requests. I was asked to speak, first to local groups, then to organizations across the country. And they actually paid me! For the first time in my life, I felt important, professional, competent, like I was finally becoming my own person.

Life was looking up. We adopted a beautiful baby girl we named Julie, and since I was rarely home, I found a fantastic nanny. I was thoroughly enjoying—and totally hooked on—this delicious new feeling of being a career woman. In the heady swirl of constant activity, my husband's gambling problem ceased to concern me.

Work can be a powerful narcotic. It numbed my pain just enough that I actually believed I was happy and all was well. Until one night, as I tucked Melissa, who was now six years old, into bed, she looked up at me with tears pooling in her big brown eyes.

"What good is it having a mommy," she said, gulping back a sob, "if she's always with clients?"

I froze. Her words felt like ice picks piercing my heart. I vowed to work less. And I did for a while. But gradually I slipped back into busyness. I was an addict, after all. I needed my fix to feel important, to deaden the pain, to let me pretend my life wasn't spiraling out of control.

Meanwhile, my secretary, Anne, was studying to be a Unity minister. She'd bring books to the office for me to read, books by Eric Butterworth, Catherine Ponder, and other Unity leaders. I devoured them like a famished lion consuming fresh meat. I was starving for the spiritual nourishment those books offered. Each page gave me hope. I wanted more.

Unity headquarters was located just outside Kansas City. When I announced one Sunday morning that I was leaving for church, my Israeli husband looked at me like I was nuts. I didn't care. I may be Jewish, but I was hurting and Unity seemed like a place where I might find solace.

Though I would never describe myself as "religious," I always considered myself "spiritual," believing in a faraway God figure. But that morning at Unity, I had an experience that forever transformed my personal connection to the Divine. During the service, the minister had us close our eyes. Then he asked, "If you had six months to live, where would you be, who would you be with, and what would you be doing?"

Instantly, I was there, I mean *really there*. I was no longer in a church pew. I was sitting on the side of a hill, overlooking water, and I was writing. I was writing a book! The experience was so real, the vision so vivid, I couldn't dismiss it. There wasn't much water and even fewer hills in Kansas City, so clearly we had to relocate. The fact that I'd never written anything other than college papers, which I never much enjoyed doing, didn't deter me a bit. I knew this vision was the answer to my prayers.

I raced home, grabbed my husband from the kitchen floor, where he was playing a game with the girls, and dragged him into the bedroom.

"We have to move," I gasped, almost breathless. "We have to live near water and I'm going to write!" Surprisingly, my husband readily agreed. Maybe he was swept away by my enthusiasm. More likely, he saw the move as an escape from reality, or at least a welcome diversion, perhaps even a chance to magically improve his perpetual losing streak.

Things fell into place surprisingly fast. Six months later, we piled into the station wagon, our girls and their hamsters in tow, en route to San Francisco. January 1, 1982, we crossed the Golden Gate Bridge into Marin County, headed for our rental home in the Tiburon hills. I'd sold my business to a friend from graduate school, Janice, who had joined me as a partner in the company. We decided we'd self-publish a job-hunting book. I'd write it. Janice would edit and handle the details.

And now, here I was, sitting on the side of a hill, overlooking water, working on a book, home for my kids. Living an answered prayer.

My husband was ecstatic too. He'd bought a seat on the Pacific Stock Exchange, which was akin to an alcoholic becoming a bartender. His drug of choice was puts and calls, complicated stock options none of which I understood. He was constantly on the phone with his bookie . . . er, broker . . . shouting orders to "Sell!" "Buy!" "Hold!" It didn't matter where we were; he'd instinctively scope out the nearest phone booth— this was before cell phones and internet investing. He didn't really care about the money. For him, trading was all about the adrenaline rush.

In the meantime, I made sure my financial blinders were firmly in place, fastened tight. I saw only what I wanted to see. I was too afraid, felt too stupid, to admit to myself that my husband's reckless behavior was putting our family at risk.

Soon after we settled in, I was standing in the checkout line at the local market. The woman behind the woman behind me was telling her companion about *A Course in Miracles*. Apparently, she'd just purchased it. My ears perked up.

"What's *A Course in Miracles*?" I asked, leaning back so I could see her.

"I'm not really sure," she said, "but it's published right here in Tiburon."

She told me where to go to buy a copy, which was only a few blocks from where I lived. Within an hour, I was the proud owner of all three volumes: the *Text*, the *Workbook*, and the *Manual for Teachers*. I'll never forget standing outside the home where I purchased them, looking reverently at the thick, heavy volumes with their dark blue hardcovers, *A Course in Miracles* embossed in gold lettering. I felt like I was holding the holy grail.

I rushed home and began reading. It quickly became apparent that this was not an easy read. The writing was dense, old-fashioned, obtuse, steeped in Christian terminology, using only male references. Yet, despite those drawbacks, I was compelled to keep going. I've been reading the *Course* almost every day now, for over thirty years.

A Course in Miracles has a beautiful backstory. Helen Schucman and William Thetford, professors of medical psychology at Columbia University College of Physicians and Surgeons, both atheists, had grown weary of the anger, tension, and strain in their department. In frustration, Bill said to Helen, "There must be another way."

His plea was like an incantation. She agreed to help him find it. Not long after, Helen sat down with pencil and paper and wrote: *"This is a course in miracles. Please take notes."*

The words came from what Helen called "the Voice." The Voice continued dictating to her for seven years as Bill typed what she wrote. In June of 1976, the twelve hundred pages he had transcribed were published in three separate volumes by the Foundation for Inner Peace.

In the beginning, I would randomly open one of the volumes and read, if not a whole page, at least various passages. Slowly bits and pieces started making sense. The *Course's* stated goal for me was "*happiness and peace*," which seemed preposterous at that point. But over time, the *Course* taught me how to shift the way I see the world, transform fear into love, and ultimately experience forgiveness.

I don't know how I would have lived through what happened next if it wasn't for the profound wisdom I found on each page.

"Every situation, properly perceived," the *Course* assured me, *"becomes an opportunity to heal."* Oh, how I longed for healing. But my husband's problem, and our marriage in particular, kept getting progressively worse.

The End of Denial

One summer day, as I stood in front of the local ATM waiting for sixty dollars in cash, the screen flashed "insufficient funds." What? I pulled my card out, shoved it back in twice, three times. The message didn't change: Sorry, no money.

That instant, I wrote a decade later in my book, *Prince Charming Isn't Coming*, was a defining moment, the moment I came out of denial.

Well, that's not quite accurate. It was merely a fleeting instant of temporary sanity before denial returned and my blinders were back on. I didn't have the courage then, when I was writing *Prince Charming*, to tell the whole story. Now I do.

That incident at the ATM would repeat itself over and over again. Each time, I'd come home enraged, and my husband would respond with gibberish. I'd stand there, my brain reeling, relying on my blinders to bring me some relief. But after numerous bouts at the ATM, those blinders began slipping off.

Between my rage and his despair, the tension at home grew intolerable. I finally asked for a divorce. He convinced me to go to counseling. Counseling didn't work. But I got pregnant. Talk about miracles! Twelve years earlier, I'd been told I'd never have more children. The divorce went on hold. My miracle baby, Anna, was born. The blinders went back on.

I stayed with him for another year, until the night he became physically abusive. That's when I left and never went back, though believe me,

I wanted to badly. I felt sorry for him. I missed him. I missed our family being together. Divorce felt wrong. I told my lawyer I only wanted a legal separation.

"Nice Jewish girls don't get divorced," I explained. She burst out laughing until she realized I was serious. She filed for divorce anyway, and I signed the papers.

My ex sued me for alimony, but my lawyer made sure that never happened. He moved back to Israel and quickly remarried.

I was left with three children, one just a baby, to raise. Fortunately, I found out my irrevocable trust fund was protected, so that even though my ex had squandered all the income, he hadn't been able to touch the principal. I still had a monthly cash flow. The financial blinders were back on in a flash. The last thing I wanted to deal with was money.

As I've said many times since, *if you don't deal with your money, your money will deal with you.* Sure enough, I soon found out I owed more than a million dollars in back taxes my ex hadn't paid and for illegal deals he got us into. My signature was on everything. I always signed whatever he gave me. My ex had left the country. I didn't have a million dollars. My lawyers pleaded "innocent spouse."

I begged my ex, a former lawyer, to write a letter to the judge explaining that I had no part in his shady deals. Instead, he sent the judge a legal brief explaining who my father was and that, of course, I was aware of everything.

The day I called my dad to ask for a loan, there was a total eclipse of the sun. Just as I heard my father's stern, unyielding "No," an eerie stillness filled the air, bathing the hills in a weird shade of green. I was sick to my stomach and utterly terrified. I felt as if I'd been abandoned by God.

Reaching for the blinders, however, was no longer an option. I wasn't going to raise my daughters on the street. But I hadn't a clue what to do. So I turned to the *Course.* It lovingly scooped me up, softly reassuring me, *"Discomfort is aroused only to bring the need for correction into awareness."*

That made sense. There was a lot in my life that needed correcting. But, as I came to see, money was just the tip of the iceberg. The *Course* said, *"A sense of separation from God is the only lack you really need to correct."*

From that minute on, my financial education became a spiritual journey. There were many pitfalls along the way, but I did my best to stay the course, leaning on those thick blue books as if they were walking sticks.

"You have no problem that He cannot solve by offering a miracle," the *Course* promised. *"You are entitled to miracles."*

That sounded good on paper. But where were the miracles when I needed them? I was struggling to keep my sanity intact and my family afloat, figure out my finances, and move forward with my life.

As I got further into the *Course*, however, I learned that miracles were nothing more than a change in perception.

Above all else, I began to pray, using words straight from the *Course*, *I want to see things differently*. Eventually I did, though it took some time, a lot of therapy, and many twelve-step meetings, like Al-Anon, Debtors Anonymous, and Co-Dependents Anonymous.

The miracle came when my eyes fixed on this passage: *"You are doing this unto yourself. That is your salvation."* As if I'd quickly turned a kaleidoscope, I saw everything in a drastically new light. This mess wasn't solely my husband's fault. I was as culpable as he. I'd given him the keys to the kingdom, abdicating all responsibility. What did I expect from an addict? I was the one enabling him.

The *Course* told me, in no uncertain terms: *"I am responsible for what I see. I choose the feelings I experience, and I decide upon the goal I would achieve. And everything that seems to happen to me I ask for, and receive as I have asked."* Quite a harsh pill to swallow, but I finally accepted that, regardless of my husband's actions, my choice to don the blinders, to be a passive victim, had created my problems. I had to start taking control.

Over time, I was able to genuinely forgive my ex and my father. Years later I actually thanked them both and truly meant it. After all, it was because of them that I discovered my calling. Once I assumed personal responsibility, my passage to financial empowerment shifted into high gear. *Prince Charming Isn't Coming* describes my entire journey, a two-pronged process combining the *Outer Work of Wealth* (learning the mechanics of money) and the *Inner Work of Wealth* (overcoming the emotional blocks).

But what I wasn't brave enough to mention in that earlier book is the prominent role the spiritual, or *Higher Work of Wealth*, played. While I steadfastly did the *Outer Work*, reading and studying, I was also lapping up every crumb the *Course* had to give me.

One night, at a Debtors Anonymous meeting, a man in a brown plaid shirt asked the group with such poignancy: "Why is it so hard? I can turn over my life to my Higher Power in every area but money."

Heads nodded in agreement, including mine. Then, a miracle occurred, a moment of clarity. Suddenly I saw my past realization—when my father refused to loan me money—much differently. God had not abandoned me. I had abandoned God. *"When you think God has not answered your call,"* declares the *Course*, *"you have not answered His."*

I Can See Clearly Now

One evening when the kids were at their friends' and I had the house to myself, I decided it was time to look at my financial statements. I'd been intentionally avoiding these documents. Even with all the studying and reading I'd been doing, just glancing at them was agonizing. My eyes would glaze over, my brain would fog up. I'd feel hopelessly stupid.

This time, however, I did as the *Course* instructed. *"Learn to be quiet, for His Voice is heard in stillness."* I sat quietly in meditation for a very long time, perhaps hours, praying for help, reminding myself, *"I need do nothing except not interfere."*

When I was done, I took a long bath, put on my favorite cream-colored chenille robe, lit some vanilla-scented candles, and sat down with the papers. I understood everything. Everything! It was like the veils had lifted. I saw that if I sold all my stocks and bonds, I could pay the tax bills, which my attorneys had negotiated down significantly. I still had real estate providing enough income to live on. I also realized if I continued to do nothing, there'd be more tax bills—or worse.

Slowly I took the financial reins, and shockingly, I started to enjoy the process.

"*Remember*," the *Course* declared, "*no one is where he is by accident, and chance plays no part in God's plan.*" That got me thinking. Could all the hardship I'd suffered have happened for a reason?

Around that time, I bumped into a friend I hadn't seen in ages. Before I'd even finished updating her, she interrupted me: "If I had your experience, I'd write a book for women about how not to get ripped off by men."

I loved the idea! By then, I'd already written *How to Become Happily Employed*, which had been picked up by Random House. I was now working as a business journalist, gaining the skills to write and, with all the studying I'd done, the knowledge to teach women about money, though I still had plenty more to learn. But as the *Course* repeatedly instructs us: "*Teach what you need to learn. No one learns more than the teacher.*" That's exactly what I longed to be doing, teaching women about money. But I didn't know where to start.

I grew impatient. I kept reminding myself what the *Course* promises: "*There is no problem in any situation that faith will not solve.*" My faith was shaky, but I clung to it as best I could. Sometimes I was barely hanging on.

Then out of the blue, I got a call from a woman at JFK University in Pleasant Hill, California. She'd heard I had a great personal story and wanted me to speak at a women's financial conference the university was hosting. You could have knocked me over with a feather. I have no idea how she found me or knew my story. I wrote for the *San Francisco Business Times* about workplace issues, not economics or finances, and definitely not my private ordeals.

I took my friend Carol Adrienne, a successful author, with me for moral support. She ran up to me after my speech, beaming with excitement. "You've got a book in there," she exclaimed, grabbing my arms, jumping up and down.

That's what I was hoping she'd say, though the idea of going public with my personal story, exposing my private humiliations, filled me with terror. Later, I randomly opened the *Course* to read: *"God's Voice asks one question only: Are you ready yet to help Me save the world?"*

Yes, I replied, I am ready. And I meant it. I had no idea at the time where this journey would take me, but I buckled up for the ride, which has been full of surprising twists and unexpected turns.

I've come a long way since then. I've touched the lives of thousands of women. Now with this, my seventh book, I stand ready again, this time ready to come out of my spiritual closet and to share what I believe to be true: the moment you inject faith into finances, the instant you invite the Divine into your relationship with the "almighty dollar," your experience with money grows deeper, richer, and more meaningful, and the results are truly profound.

I've even coined a word for this work, *metafiscal—that which blends financial know-how with metaphysical principles; a melding of the spiritual and the practical in regard to money.*

You don't have to be religious to be *metafiscal.* I'm certainly not. But I do agree with Deepak Chopra, who said, "We need a more spiritual approach to success and to affluence." Even our founding fathers made sure "In God We Trust" was emblazoned on our currency. God can be whatever you're comfortable with—a personified deity, a Higher Power, your inner wisdom, or an all-encompassing energy far greater than our earthly selves.

For some of you, it may seem odd, if not off-putting, to say the word "money" in the same breath as God. After all, the Bible tells us that the love of money is the root of all evil. But the fact is, money itself is not bad. Nor is it good. As the *Course* reminds us, *"Money is not evil. It is nothing."* Money is just a bunch of paper and metal. Money can't shoot a gun. Or bandage a wound. Only people can. It's not the love of money that's the problem. It's the lack of self-love that leads to trouble. Evil stems from fear, insecurity, and self-hatred. Prosperity is a by-product of self-love, self-worth, self-respect.

I truly believe money is God made visible. When you treat your money with the reverence and respect it deserves, it will shower endless blessings upon you, allowing you to serve others for all your days and beyond.

My intention in writing this book is to help you create financial miracles. And to show you that, even with money, *especially* with money, when you develop a deep sense of trust in the inexplicable forces of the Universe, along with learning the practical facts, everything changes. Financial success becomes a transformational journey, a personal healing, a sacred initiation, empowering you to become all you're meant to be and to do what you're put on this planet to do.

Sacred Success wasn't easy for me to write and took over seven years to complete. Yet it never occurred to me to give up, at least not for very long. I couldn't. I'd said "yes" to God.

Best-Laid Plans

Actually, the book I started writing was worlds away from what you're reading now. Initially, I intended to write about women who make millions. The idea came when I set a new goal for myself: "Make millions, help millions, give millions."

Sure, the thought of making seven figures was a bit daunting. But I knew exactly what to do. I'd start by interviewing women who were making millions. That was how I had finally made six figures, by interviewing high earners, then writing a book, *Secrets of Six-Figure Women*.

Buoyed by my impressive new goal—*make millions, help millions, give millions*—I plunged into the research, eager to uncover the keys to the seven-figure club. Finding ultra-high earners was surprisingly easy. Interviewing them was fascinating. I was totally smitten with this project. I wrote a proposal, submitted it to publishers, and waited with eager anticipation for their replies. Every editor turned it down.

Just as the country was beginning to rebound from the Great Recession, I slipped into my own emotional slump. Nowhere near my lofty goal, devastated by the rejections, I admitted defeat. But the book wasn't ready to give up on me. My intuition kept stubbornly insisting that something in those interviews needed to be shared, but either I wasn't expressing it adequately or I'd missed it completely.

I was stuck, bordering on burnout, but not in the classic sense. I wasn't exhausted or depressed. I was just "blah," as if there was no creative juice left in this orange. I'd lost my passion for my work, which threw me for a loop. Mine was more than a career, it was a labor of love, a spiritual calling, a personal ministry.

When I shared this with my business coach, Martha Lynn Mangum, she suggested I take a break. "You're too into doing, Barbara," she said. "You need time for just being." I knew she was right. I made reservations that afternoon for a much-needed four-day getaway.

The next morning, I headed to a cozy lodge overlooking the waters of the Hood Canal, about a two-hour drive from my home. I arranged spa appointments for every afternoon. Otherwise, I stayed in my room, curled up on the window seat, rereading my interviews, praying for guidance, ordering room service.

"A healed mind does not plan," the *Course* explains. *"It carries out the plan it receives through listening to Wisdom that is not its own."*

I was hoping to receive some of that Wisdom. But I figured, at the very least, I'd return home with relaxed muscles, painted nails, and freshly waxed brows.

Giving Birth

Four days later, I departed with far more wisdom than I ever could have imagined. Something totally unexpected occurred on the very first morning, kept happening throughout my stay, and continued for months after I returned home. I started receiving what I fondly referred to as "Downloads from the Divine."

Sometimes these messages came through a hushed voice in my head; other times, they showed up while I was writing in my journal. There were mornings I'd awaken at the crack of dawn with a flood of fully formed, though brand-new-to-me, concepts careening through my brain.

I recorded everything in my journal. Seeds were being planted that, given time, would sprout into a new body of work. I called this work *Sacred Success*, the name courtesy of one of those Divine Downloads. Much of what I wrote during those four days appears throughout this book, beginning in Chapter 3.

While most of my ideas were far from fully developed, the blahs vanished, and my energy returned. I came back from my retreat with a whole new respect for downtime. I began looking at my life with fresh eyes, through the filter of *Sacred Success*, and I began applying what I'd learned to my own experiences. Less than a year later, I was giving teleclasses and lectures to test out the material. Eventually I was offering four-day *Sacred Success* retreats on both coasts.

Two things became exquisitely clear. I saw how profoundly trans-formational this work was, for me and for my students. And I knew *Sacred Success*, the book I would be writing, had absolutely nothing to do with making millions. It wasn't even really about money, for that matter. At its very core, *Sacred Success* was about power.

What This Book Is *Really* About

In observing my own progress, studying my interviews, and working with my clients and students, I came to realize that financial success, for women, is a Rite of Passage into our power (more about this in Chapter 2). Historically, Rites of Passage were used to mark and give meaning to a person's transition from one status to another. The transition we're marking is the shift from dependency to autonomy, from reliant child to responsible adult. In the transition ritual, sacred wisdom was passed on by a tribal elder.

I, the tribal elder, have written *Sacred Success* for every woman—from full-time moms to management executives, from solopreneurs to CEOs—who hungers for more. Not just to make more money, but to live a more meaningful life.

My purpose, in writing this book, is threefold. I intend to:

1. Reveal the Feminine Face of Power, giving you permission to raise your sights higher, stay true to yourself, and stimulate discussion on the impact you can have and the legacy you wish to leave.

2. Guide you through this Rite of Passage, step by step, with powerful exercises and guided visualizations that I use in my retreats, to take you deeper into the process. Throughout the book, you'll be accompanied by others who've taken the journey. These women will tell you, in their own words, how they transformed their lives and how you can do the same.

3. Ask you the question that was so provocative for me: *Are you ready yet to help save the world?* I truly believe our hope for the future lies with powerful women: women who know who they are and express that in the world, women who speak up instead of holding their tongues, women who do what they fear instead of staying where it's safe, women who are financially responsible and economically independent.

The fact that this book found its way into your hands suggests that you've already answered the question—yes, you are ready for *Sacred Success*.

I predict that as the tenets of *Sacred Success* become more widely known and practiced, we'll see women's levels of influence soar exponentially. And because of women's increasing impact, in partnership with enlightened men, it will be fascinating to watch how the global landscape shifts.

I recall the late New York congresswoman Bella Abzug's prediction: "In the twenty-first century, women will change the nature of power rather than power changing the nature of women." That's exactly what *Sacred Success* sets out to do.

PART ONE

The Problem

CHAPTER 1

Women, Wealth, and Power . . . Oh My!

"Limitless power is God's gift to you, because it is what you are."

—A Course in Miracles

The New Game of Money

"All wealth is the offspring of power."

—Charles F. Haanel

I begin this chapter reminded of a saying: *Want to make God laugh? Tell Her your plans.* God must surely be cracking up as I sit here typing. This is not the book I intended to write. But like so much in life, to paraphrase John Lennon, it's what happened while I was busy making other plans.

My "other" plan was to write about women who make millions, as I mentioned in the introduction. However, after interviewing scores of extremely high earners, I began to observe something I hadn't expected. These women were playing a very different game with some surprising new rules. The fact that the women I interviewed were earning such substantial sums was not nearly as significant as the *way* they were doing it.

The real revelation was how powerful each successful woman had become. Not because the money gave her power, but because, by reclaiming her power, she was able to maximize her wealth. These women were showing me a radically new paradigm of power.

I could've kicked myself for not seeing it sooner.

I've spent my entire career helping women financially. Much remains the same in the decades since I first started. The whopping majority of us still earn far less than men, live in higher levels of poverty, and tend to ignore or neglect our finances, putting ourselves at serious economic risk.

Granted, times are changing. Today women control more money than ever before. A Family Wealth Advisors Council study in 2012 revealed that females now hold 51.3 percent, or $14 trillion, of personal wealth, and that figure is expected to grow to $22 trillion within the next decade. And according to the latest US census, 22 percent of women outearn their male partners, another number predicted to increase.

Good news, however, can be deceiving. Many of these very women are standing on dangerously thin ice. Just because a woman has money, as I experienced myself, doesn't mean she'll keep it, enjoy it, or use it wisely. Studies consistently show that women, though they may know better and desire otherwise, are not protecting themselves financially. The recognition is there, but their resistance is stronger.

This is true even for women who work in the financial industry. I can't tell you how many mortgage brokers, insurance executives, chief financial officers, and investment advisors come up to me after a speech and say in total embarrassment, "I do this for a living but my own finances are a wreck," or "I manage millions of dollars, but when it comes to my checkbook, I feel like a klutz."

I've known, ever since I healed my own relationship with money and began researching my first financial book in 1995, that women's resistance to dealing with money has far less to do with the fundamentals of finance than with their fear of (or ambivalence about) power.

Take my marriage to the gambler. I had the money, but he had the power. I gave it to him by deferring all the decisions. I was too scared to speak up, take control, or even try to educate myself financially.

Phyllis Chesler said it this way in her groundbreaking book *Women, Money, and Power*: "Money is a power sacred to most men and foreign to most women." Though she wrote those words more than thirty years ago, they still ring true today.

More recently, in her 2013 book, *The End of Men*, Hanna Rosin observed: "The closer women get to real power, the more they cling to the idea they are powerless."

My biggest challenge, as a coach and teacher, is getting women past their own often fierce resistance to making, managing, or simply understanding money. "It isn't about money," I'll tell them. "It's about power." They nod, knowingly but cautiously, as if I'm describing a desirable location they aren't quite ready to visit.

In speeches, I often ask women, "What's the first thought that comes to mind when I say the word 'power'?" With notable exceptions, their responses aren't pretty. Many associate power with control and domination, with backstabbing and battling for position, with acting like a bitch or turning into a male clone. I see the same sentiment in the media.

"It is not becoming for a woman to think about power," a female venture capitalist told *Fast Company* magazine recently. "To enjoy power is to enjoy control, especially over other people." Similarly, a female executive quoted in the *Kansas City Star* said, "Power is a description of a person who's egotistical and self-directed."

This attitude isn't just confined to the workplace, as Jenna Goudreau points out in a *ForbesWoman* blog post, "Why Successful Women Terrify Us": "Lifestyle magazines and romantic comedies also often paint power in women as threatening, especially when it comes to love. Female success scares men away, they taunt. It's intimidating, abnormal and unattractive. But if you just *have to* earn more than him, do let him drive and don't talk about work. How generous."

Not surprising, then, that in a 2012 study, *Women and the Paradox of Power*, 38 percent of respondents said they'd rather be well-liked than powerful. As if the two were mutually exclusive.

Power Is Scary

> "Between the ages of 9 to 15, girls lose who they are, they lose who they want to be, and become what society wants."
>
> —Marie Wilson

Our confusion around power should come as no surprise. Historically, girls haven't been groomed, expected, or encouraged to be successful, powerful adults. If anything, we were raised as the power behind the throne, often punished for even aspiring higher.

"Behind every successful man, there's always a woman," my mother would say, beaming with pride, as I was growing up. Later, both my parents criticized me harshly when I started a business instead of staying home with my kids. Every day was an internal battle between social-ization and self-determination, between guilt and ambition, between cultural mores and my authentic desires.

Thankfully, times have changed dramatically. Yet even younger generations—who may have societal permission to do it all—are still largely hardwired to hold back, or are exhausted from doing too much. And there's a dearth of role models to show them the ropes or prove that it's possible or permissible. Even today, many women are victims of the still-prevailing patriarchy.

Sheryl Sandberg, forty-five, chief operating officer of Facebook, comments in her book, *Lean In*, "We internalize the negative mes-sages we get throughout our lives, the messages that say it's wrong to be outspoken, aggressive, more powerful than men. We lower our own expectations of what we can achieve."

I vividly remember a woman in her early thirties telling me she'd gone into counseling, frustrated by her lack of success, only to realize she hadn't been taking herself seriously as a professional. When pressed by her therapist, she sheepishly confessed, "Maybe I don't want to grow up, be a powerful adult, able to effect what I want in my life."

I had to ask, "So what's your payoff for not being powerful?"

She paused. "The thing that just came to me was that I get an excuse. But that's kind of twisted because it's certainly not a real benefit."

Later, while pondering her response, it occurred to me that maybe her thinking wasn't so twisted. Maybe our collective unconscious has been molded by centuries of conditioning. Maybe avoidance of power *has been beneficial*, a means of survival for the female of the species. As psychologist Olivia Mellan once told me, "Powerful women have been burned at the stake."

Her words sent shivers up my spine. I'm convinced that beneath our dislike of or discomfort with power lurks a deeper, more ominous concern—the dire consequences we might suffer if we become truly powerful. Historical narratives of strong, assertive, outspoken women being severely punished have permeated our collective unconscious.

Somewhere along the way, financial incompetence became a safe house of sorts, granting us protection and, oddly enough, security. Think about it. There's no better way to limit our power than by lowering our earning potential or by mishandling, neglecting, or ignoring our money.

In the words of Alice Walker, author of *The Color Purple*, "The most common way people give up their power is by thinking they don't have any." *A Course in Miracles* says it even more plainly: "*Do you not see that all your misery comes from the strange belief that you are powerless?*"

Until recently, society was all too happy to collude with that charade. It wasn't until 1975 that women were allowed to have credit cards and open bank accounts in their own names, without a male cosigner.

Even today, some churches condemn "filthy lucre," and you'll still hear "New Agers" preaching the nobility of poverty.

This explains why even a number of those women I interviewed, who eventually made millions, were at some point conflicted or confused about money. Marsha Firestone, president and founder of the prestigious Women Presidents' Organization, whose members average $13 million in annual revenue, told me that one of the biggest issues for these women is how much to pay themselves. "Eventually they learn to pay themselves a lot. But they have to learn it's okay to make a lot of money, and to be proud of it."

Quite a few admitted as much to me: "I had to learn it was all right for me to have money and success, even more than I could imagine. That it's right, not wrong, to be prosperous," said one.

"I had mixed feelings around money," confessed another. "I wanted more, but was it okay to have it? Once I got that it was, the money came so fast."

Until we give ourselves the same permission to prosper, we remain well-trained victims or master manipulators, acquiring our clout through compliance or charm, shedding tears or fluttering lashes, or through eruptions of fury and icy cold shoulders—all forms of cheap (not genuine) power, with disastrous effects on our self-esteem.

"The traditional female means of power—beauty and attachment to boys—radically reduces their self-worth," declares Marie Wilson, founder of The White House Project, in her book, *Closing the Leadership Gap.*

Indeed, low self-worth is the major culprit in most cases of financial inertia. Our feminine psyche, operating like a highly sensitive sonar system, emits subtle warnings, inexplicable waves of trepidation, when we get too close to rocking the boat. To avoid making waves, we water ourselves down.

We weren't born this way. Studies show that both sexes are equally aggressive until age four. "But as they get older, girls are pressured and expected to please everyone while boys are encouraged to be assertive, tough, and strong," points out Joyce Roché, former CEO of Girls, Inc. "What's troubling is that girls aren't taught to pursue power in a positive way."

Or as famed anthropologist Mary Catherine Bateson put it, "Our society has actually cultivated female weakness."

Isn't it time we start cultivating female clout? Isn't it time we start teaching women and girls how to pursue power in a positive, authentic way?

Sharing the Secret Wisdom of Women's Power

"If someone said: 'What is the reason we are born?' I would say this: 'We are born to manage power.'"

—Caroline Myss

The problem, as I see it, is this: *We've never been taught the secret wisdom of creating wealth and wielding power—as women.* For centuries women have come together to trade recipes and remedies, share tips on attracting a man or raising a child. But there is little, if any, collective wisdom for wealth and power, success and ambition.

In my experience, women are ravenous for this information. When Health Alliance Plan, an HMO with 500,000 members, asked women, "What is the single biggest challenge that's holding you back from living Your Perfect Life?" the whopping majority (29 percent) said money. (The runners-up: time, 24 percent; confidence, 17 percent; health, 16 percent.)

Sacred Success is meant to be part of an ongoing tradition of women sharing their wisdom, with a new generation of role models who've stepped into their power *on their own terms* and in a very different way than men have been doing it for centuries.

In the first blush of the feminist revolution, as women poured into the workplace, they found themselves entering alien territory, a land created by men, ruled by men, and unfriendly, if not downright hostile, to the opposite sex. Ambitious women were branded "alpha females," "pushy broads," or just plain "bitches," marginalized by men, often spurned by women, and worst of all, alienated from their authentic selves. Power quickly became a pejorative term when applied to women. And it remains so to this day.

Management studies consistently show that men who are forceful and assertive receive high marks and respect from their bosses. Women who are forceful and assertive are downgraded, belittled, or rebuffed.

"Women still have an uneasy relationship with power," Arianna Huffington noted in a 2007 *Newsweek* story, "Women and Power." "There is this internalized fear that if we are really powerful, we are going to be considered ruthless or pushy or strident—all those epithets that strike right at our femininity. We are still working at trying to overcome the fear that power and womanliness are mutually exclusive."

Few women have been raised to believe that achieving wealth and power on their own is even an option—short of marrying a tycoon or top-tiered politician. Achieving it themselves, by the sweat of their brow or the brilliance of their ideas, seems—well, ridiculous, or debilitating.

Admittedly, many women have attained economic success in the male system, but it usually comes at an appalling price. In 2003, *New York Times* reporter Lisa Belkin sparked a media frenzy when she coined the phrase "the opt-out revolution" to describe the flood of women exiting the workforce. In order to sustain a high level of success, along with a quality life, they could no longer continue to push themselves unmercifully, as many of their male colleagues were doing. They were no longer willing to stay in a system that rewarded the sacrifice of self for the sake of success.

But I believe that what the media defined as women opting out was, in large part, *women waking up*. Women were beginning to question the status quo, realizing *there must be another way* to stay true to themselves and be well paid, without selling their souls, surrendering their authenticity, or sacrificing their values.

Redefining the P Word

"We fear and crave becoming truly ourselves."

—Abraham Maslow

Whatever the reason, the sexes view power through very different lenses. A 2012 Simmons School of Management study concluded, "Women tend to interpret and enact power differently from men." And here's the difference: Women make things happen by building relationships, men by asserting control. Women work best in collaborative models of *"power with,"* while men tend to conduct business in a hierarchical model of *"power over."*

Generally speaking, a man's self-esteem comes from his achievements; power itself is the ultimate goal. A woman, deriving her self-esteem from relationships, considers power a means to an end.

Once a woman realizes that her viewpoint is equally valid, power takes on a more positive spin. Rather than instinctively recoiling in fear, she genuinely relishes and eagerly pursues power, as if, to borrow from Anaïs Nin, remaining a tight bulb becomes more painful than the risk it takes to blossom.

"If we fully express who we are, we are said to be 'full of power,'" author Angeles Arrien said. "When we demonstrate our power, no one can tell us what can't be done."

The word "power," which comes from the Latin word *potere* ("to be able"), means *the ability to act or produce an effect.* The definition applies to both genders. But as it relates to women, I much prefer to define power using the words of renowned psychologist Erich Fromm: *"The main task in life is to give birth to our self to become what we actually are."*

That task is the essence of power, the ultimate reason for creating wealth, the essential challenge facing women today. It's each woman becoming who she is meant to be, the ultimate authority in her life, that allows her to accumulate wealth and use it as a tool to increase her choices, improve her circumstances, follow her calling, help those she loves, and turn this planet into a better place.

"The path to my success was never about attaining incredible wealth or celebrity," media mogul Oprah Winfrey admitted. "It was about the process of continually seeking to be better, challenging myself to pursue excellence on every level. The whole point of being alive is to evolve into the complete person you were intended to be."

When you view power from that angle, you begin to understand our resistance more clearly. *Essentially, our fear of power is our fear of becoming who we really are.* This fear keeps us settling for less instead of striving for more, shrinking to fit rather than playing full out, clinging to safety to avoid taking the leap.

As I've said before, money does not give us power. But it does give us choices. Our power comes from the choices we make, choices that reflect who we are, not what someone else wants; choices that accelerate our growth, not accommodate others. Ultimately, *claiming our power is an act of individuation*, distinguishing what's true for us from what's been artificially imposed—by our family or society as a whole—then letting go of what no longer serves us. What we think we are supposed to be—all the *shoulds, oughts, musts*—too often gets in the way of what we actually could be.

"I tried so hard to fit myself into a mold of what I thought I should be. I never stopped to figure out who I was and work with that," said one highly successful woman about a low point in her past.

And another told me: "I feel like I've spent my whole life in denial, not just about my money, but about who I really am. I've had to come out of denial to tell the truth."

Too many women are still living in denial and self-deception. *Sacred Success* intends to radically change that by redefining power. A powerful woman is *someone who knows who she is, knows what she wants, and expresses that in the world, unapologetically.*

As Maria Shriver once explained to a reporter, "True power is about being true to yourself and finding your own voice and path in the world." For many of us, as Shriver admits, our efforts to gain "more conscious awareness of the power that lies within" has been a lifelong endeavor.

The *Paradox of Sacred Success*: It's Not about Money

"Only your misperceptions stand in your way."

—*A Course in Miracles*

When I was interviewing mega–high earners, I'd been so dazzled by their outrageous financial success (and my eagerness to replicate it) that I had failed to notice that these women were sharing more than their financial prowess. They were showing me the Feminine Face of Wealth and Power, which was considerably different from what the male world models. Here's why.

By and large, men are very motivated by profit, perks, prestige. For men, the promise of affluence is a powerful incentive. But it's different for women. Unless she's in the throes of survival, struggling to put food on the table, a woman is rarely motivated by money alone. What motivates her, most often, is the opportunity to help others.

A Simmons School of Management survey confirms that more than 70 percent of women polled report they are driven not by "perks, position, or personal gain," but by the desire to help others, contribute to communities, and make the world a better place.

These are two very different paths: "Show me the money" versus "Show me how to help." Sure, most women must work to make a living, but at the same time, many—including those who aren't gainfully employed, like full-time moms, volunteers, and retirees—yearn to play a bigger, more meaningful game. This is the game I call *Sacred Success*. This game has a decidedly spiritual component and a deep commitment to a higher purpose, or as several women called it, a "search for significance."

I define *Sacred Success* as *pursuing your Soul's purpose for your own bliss and the benefit of others, while being richly rewarded.* The goal isn't to "finish rich" (though that may be a desired result) but to become the powerful force you were born to be. That's precisely where I had veered off course. I was so fixated on profit, I never noticed there was a paradox in play, what I call the *Paradox of Sacred Success.*

As a recovered underearner myself, I had written a book about and spent the last decade teaching *Overcoming Underearning* classes. The greatest hurdle, for an underearner, is accepting that it's okay to profit, not an easy or comfortable task for many women. However—here's the paradox—in *Sacred Success*, profit is no longer the primary goal. The primary goal is achieving Greatness. Greatness is fueled by passion, by purpose, by doing what you were born to do. It's why you're here. It's the truth of who you are. It's what your Soul yearns for. And it's what the world desperately needs. Greatness is where your *real* power resides.

Money is not an end, but serves as a means to an end, a tool for creating a meaningful life. The women who made millions were telling me, "*Yes, there is another way*": merging higher incomes with a higher calling, and playing the game according to their feminine nature, deepest truths, and personal missions.

They definitely intended to be financially rewarded, but money was not their driving force. What drove them was their desire to reach their fullest potential and make an impact on this planet. "I'm not doing this for the money," many told me, often chastising me for suggesting they were.

Indeed, I see the same reactions with most clients I coach or those I teach. Tell a woman she can substantially increase her income, and she may get excited about the possibility, but not enough to stretch beyond her comfort zone, a prerequisite for financial success. However, tell her that having more money enables her to make a difference in the lives of those she loves, or contribute to causes she cares about, and she'll light up like Christmas, ablaze with the determination and the daring to do whatever it takes, despite fear and self-doubt, spurring her to be and do more than any paycheck ever could.

I realized that this was a constant theme in my interviews with women making millions. They rarely accumulated wealth for material gain. They did it for what wealth meant in its original Latin: "well-being." Their focus (and their motivation) derived from how well they could serve.

Clothing designer Nina McLemore is a good example. Her accessories company was purchased by Liz Claiborne in 1986, and by 1993 Nina was the top-ranking woman in the company. She told me, "I really wanted to support women in the arts, so I made a conscious decision to put some of my assets at risk to start a new business. The goal was to make more money so that I could not only have financial security, but enough money for philanthropy."

So too, when I asked venture capitalist Christine Comaford, a former Buddhist monk who founded six high-tech companies and was one of the early funders of Google, what fueled her incredible financial success, she didn't miss a beat: "What drives me is making a difference, making a contribution, giving money away."

Why Is *Sacred Success* Important?

"To be yourself in a world that is constantly trying to make you something else is the greatest accomplishment."

—Ralph Waldo Emerson

Reclaiming our "true power" is not by any means an issue affecting only women. It has global ramifications. I believe *when enough women build sizable fortunes and understand how to ply their power, the whole world will profit.*

Consider this: Even though men earn more, women are far bigger contributors to charity. "High-income producing women ... give significantly more to noble causes than do their male counterparts," wrote Thomas Stanley in *Millionaire Women Next Door*. And a recent study by the Women's Philanthropy Institute at the University of Indiana found women are as much as 40 percent more likely to donate than men.

An interesting fact: Studies show that the sexes differ in their approach to philanthropy. The top three reasons men give are to have a building named after them, respond to pressure from office or peers, or get a seat on the board. The top three reasons women give are to make a difference, pass on family tradition, and give back to community.

The planet desperately needs more financially empowered women. As the Dalai Lama famously observed, "The world will be saved by the Western woman." Add to that Mother Teresa's statement, "It takes a checkbook to change the world."

A few years ago, a headline on Businessweek.com caught my eye: "Is the Financial Crisis a Male Syndrome?" "Could it be," the authors ask, "that male domination of market finance results in excessive speculation and risk-taking at the expense of global stability?"

The authors—both men, I might add—admitted that too much testosterone is running the world, leading to greater aggression, Machiavellian risk-taking, repeated wars, and financial meltdowns.

I especially like the way Elizabeth Warren described the 2008–2009 economic fiasco in an interview with the *Boston Globe*: "There really is an element—at least in this crisis—about how the 'Old Boys Club' brought us not just to the brink of ruin, but beyond that, and how they still want to play the same way. And somebody's got to say 'No.'"

I believe when enough powerful women in partnership with enlightened men come together, we'll have the resources, values, vision, sensitivity, and courage to loudly, proudly, and decisively say no to the "Old Boys Club," paving the way to saner solutions for healing this planet and changing this world.

Both Sexes Benefit

> *"Everyone is looking for himself and for the power and glory he thinks he's lost."*
>
> —*A Course in Miracles*

Let me be very clear. I am not waving the banner of female superiority or bashing men in any way. In fact, I'm hoping this book helps men better understand the Feminine Face of Power. I believe they are as afraid of our power as we are! One high earner may have nailed it when she told me, "I think men are afraid that if you give a woman too much power, we'll skewer them in public one day."

Men need to know we're not seeking domination for ourselves, submission from them, or any form of retribution. That's not how we roll. We want to share power, not usurp it. Remember, we want power "with," not power "over." We are seeking a better way that respects gender differences but repudiates gender typecasting, giving everyone the right to go after their dreams in whatever ways feel genuinely compelling, personally satisfying, and mutually enriching.

It is my belief that, as you courageously step into your authentic power, letting your light shine despite your trepidation, you will inspire countless others—male and female—to do the same.

CHAPTER SUMMARY: Women, Wealth, and Power . . . Oh My!

- Women's difficulties with money have far less to do with the fundamentals of finance than with their fear of (or ambivalence about) power.

- Beneath our dislike of or discomfort with power lurks a deeper, more ominous concern—the dire consequences we might suffer if we become truly powerful.

- There's no better way to limit our power than by lowering our earning potential or by mishandling, neglecting, or ignoring our money.

- The problem is this: *We've never been taught the secret wisdom of creating wealth and wielding power—as women.*

- Whatever the reason, the sexes view power through very different lenses.

- For men, power itself is the ultimate goal. Women consider power a means to an end.

- The definition of power, as it relates to women, can be summed up in the words of psychologist Erich Fromm: "*The main task in life is to give birth to our self to become what we actually are.*"

- Essentially, our fear of power is our fear of becoming who we really are.

- A powerful woman is *someone who knows who she is, knows what she wants, and expresses that in the world, unapologetically.*

- Powerful women are playing a very different game I call *Sacred Success*. While men are very motivated by profit, perks, and prestige, women are driven by the opportunity to help others and the desire to play a bigger, more meaningful game.

- The definition of *Sacred Success: pursuing your Soul's purpose for your own bliss and the benefit of others, while being richly rewarded.*

- The *Paradox of Sacred Success*—profit is no longer the primary goal. The primary goal is achieving Greatness, fueled by your passion and purpose.

- Money is not an end, but a tool for creating a meaningful life.

- As you courageously step into your authentic power, you will inspire countless others—male and female—to do the same.

CHAPTER 2

Preparing for the Passage

"This is a course in mind training."

—*A Course in Miracles*

A Parable

"In the beginner's mind there are many possibilities, but in the expert's there are few."

—*Shunryu Suzuki*

Before we embark on our Rite of Passage, becoming privy to the secret wisdom of women's power, let me begin with a story.

Once upon a time, a seeker came to Buddha, wanting the master to teach him everything he knew about life. Buddha silently studied the seeker, then turned and fetched two cups, both filled with liquid.

"The first cup," Buddha told the seeker, "represents all of your knowledge about life. The second cup represents all of my knowledge about life. If you want to fill your cup with my knowledge, you must first empty your cup of your knowledge."

And so I say to you, dear reader: By picking up this book, you've asked me to teach you everything I know about *Sacred Success*. Are you willing to empty your cup of everything *you* know about wealth and power?

"*True learning*," the *Course* tells us, is really "*unlearning*."

The more willing you are to empty your cup of preconceived beliefs and assumptions, the greater are your chances of reaching your peak potential and utmost prosperity.

What Is *Sacred Success*?

"Pray for potatoes with a hoe in your hand."

—Irish proverb

Remember, *Sacred Success* means *pursuing your Soul's purpose for your own bliss and the benefit of others, while being richly rewarded. Sacred Success* is both a practical process and a spiritual practice, equally sacred and mundane, divinely guided while grounded in action.

Sacred Success is the product of my interviews (with women who made millions, along with the graduates of my retreat), my own experience applying what I learned from those women and teaching it to others, my thirty-plus years as a student of *A Course in Miracles*, and, of course, my Downloads from the Divine.

The Four Core Principles

"All of Life is an exercise in strengthening the mind."

—Mark Fisher

In one of the Downloads that came to me two weeks before my first *Sacred Success* retreat, I received the Four Core Principles of Wealth and Power that are vital to *Sacred Success*:

1. Financial well-being is essential to achieving Greatness.
2. Our financial foundation is only as strong as our individual integrity.

3. Power demands responsibility.

4. Our power comes from one of two sources—Love or Fear.

These Core Principles are the foundation on which your power rests. Whenever you flip into fear, feel like you're stuck, or find yourself struggling, immediately revisit these principles. I promise, at least one of these four is out of kilter. And I can assure you, this is not about being perfect, which is neither possible nor desirable. It's about being persistent.

(Note: One of the more fascinating aspects of my downloads was that the information usually came in groups of four. One day, while typing up the workbook for my retreat, I accidentally hit the shift button and the number *4* at the same time. Do you know what happens when you capitalize a *4*? It turns into the dollar sign: $.)

1. FINANCIAL WELL-BEING IS ESSENTIAL TO ACHIEVING GREATNESS.

"Economic security is the foundation of power."

—*Martin Luther King Jr.*

As I've said, making a lot of money is not the primary goal of *Sacred Success*, though it's often a by-product. The primary goal is achieving Greatness, which means pursuing what you were born to do as a powerful woman.

Nonetheless, money and power are inextricably linked. Financial stability is necessary to reduce any distractions to reaching Greatness. You cannot possibly follow your God-given destiny if you're drowning in debt or struggling to make ends meet. Or as prosperity author Edwene Gaines points out: "God is not served by you being poor."

Sacred Success requires you to become a good steward of your money. Not a perfect steward: No matter how good your finances, there are always challenges and concerns. But a healthy respect for money makes a considerable difference in creating financial miracles.

To begin with, *Sacred Success* requires financial solvency. So if you're in debt, you must stop using credit cards, stick to a repayment plan, spend less than you make, and consistently save (even small amounts) for emergencies (a shoe sale is not an emergency!). Nothing will get in the way of pursuing your Soul's purpose faster and more thoroughly than financial instability.

I highly recommend Debtors Anonymous (www.debtorsanonymous .org), a twelve-step program that will utterly transform your financial life. The key is to attend ninety meetings in ninety days. The good news: DA also has phone meetings.

2. OUR FINANCIAL FOUNDATION IS ONLY AS STRONG AS OUR INDIVIDUAL INTEGRITY.

> *"Self-deception is dishonesty."*
>
> —A Course in Miracles

I believe our world is moving into a whole new paradigm (more about that in Chapter 9) where integrity is sacrosanct to success. Look back at the last financial meltdown. So much of it was the direct result of a lack of integrity among individuals and institutions alike. Without integrity, no one is too big to fail. With integrity, no one is too small to soar.

The word "integrity" comes from a Latin root, meaning *wholeness* or *entirety*. Integrity demands that your words and deeds consistently reflect your deepest truths, highest aspirations, and most cherished values. Or as the *Course* puts it, "*There is nothing you say that contradicts what you think or do.*"

Whenever you're not being true to yourself, not saying what you need, making excuses, rationalizing your behavior, telling half-truths, or flat-out lying (especially to yourself), you're giving your power away. Conversely, you take your power back by identifying, verbalizing, and consistently living your truth, moment by moment. Admittedly, this requires constant vigilance. It's as easy for us to slip out of integrity as it is for a dieter to slip in extra calories, never even realizing that's what we're doing.

3. POWER DEMANDS RESPONSIBILITY.

"Power without responsibility is tyranny. Responsibility without power becomes frustration of potential."

—*Jach Pursel*

Power is rooted in what I call the Defining Truth: *No one is doing this to me. I am doing it to myself. Therefore, I have the ability to change it.*

You forfeit your power every time you point your finger—blaming others or outside conditions, allowing another to decide for you, or waiting, hoping someone or something will save you, be it Prince Charming or the lottery. You take power back by holding yourself accountable.

"Recognizing this is a crucial step in the reawakening," the *Course* says, then adds a warning: *"It is often quite painful . . . for as blame is withdrawn from without there is a strong tendency to harbor it within."*

Cheap power—like anger (especially if it's self-directed), control, domination, and manipulation—is not to be confused with authentic power (knowing who you are, what you want, and expressing that in the world, unapologetically).

4. POWER COMES FROM ONE OF TWO SOURCES— LOVE OR FEAR.

"Your choice is determined by what you value."

—*A Course in Miracles*

Imagine a loud, prolonged drumroll, to signify the monumental importance of this final principle.

Each source has a distinct voice, one genuine, the other false. The Ego is the voice of Fear, or false power. The Soul is the voice of Love, or true, genuine power. The Soul and the Ego have conflicting agendas, thus they produce dramatically different results. How can you tell the difference between the two?

The Ego's job is to keep you safe. The Ego learned its job very early in life, when you were a little tot trying to figure out the best way to avoid punishment, rejection, or disapproval. The Ego is all about self-protection and survival. But know this: The coping mechanisms you used to survive as a child will suffocate you as an adult.

The Soul doesn't care about "protecting" you. The Soul's job is to make sure you soar. The Soul, which gets its marching orders directly from the Divine, pushes you to do what you're here to do. The Soul will just as soon shove you off the cliff, if that's what it takes, knowing full well you'll fly.

The Ego focuses on your flaws. The Soul reminds you of your gifts. The Ego urges you to hide. The Soul insists that you shine. The Ego analyzes. The Soul accepts. What the Ego sees as selfish, the Soul knows is "self-fullness."

The Ego sees every person as someone from the past, reacting, as the *Course* says, "*to the present as if it were the past.*" The Soul sees everyone and everything as a mirror, a teacher, a gift from the Source.

You know your Ego is speaking when you hear yourself growing defensive or impatient, making excuses or justifying the status quo, or comparing yourself with others and either falling short or feeling superior. The Ego craves the comfort of the familiar. It is threatened by the capriciousness of the unknown. The Ego functions like an electric fence, keeping you safely ensconced in the confines of the familiar, even if it causes you pain.

Which Are You Going to Feed?

"There is no need to learn through pain."

—A Course in Miracles

There's an old Cherokee legend that says two wolves sit at our door. One is filled with fear, jealously, resentment, inferiority, greed, and lies. It will destroy us. The other is overflowing with love, joy, peace, compassion, and possibility. It will empower us. Which one is dominant depends on which one we feed. We feed one or the other depending on which we give our attention to, whose directives we heed.

Which voice are you going to feed—the Ego or the Soul? You are in control. And you cannot follow two masters. The Ego aspires to mediocrity; the Soul, to Greatness. Only the Soul is privy to the secrets of *Sacred Success*. Only the Soul is the source of true, authentic power.

"There is no compromise between the two," A Course in Miracles warns. *"If one is real, the other must be false."*

In order to convince you it's real, the Ego *always* speaks first and loudest and it never shuts up. Never! Don't even try to stifle it, because that's part of its devious plan. The Ego depends on the distraction of addictions—from alcohol or drugs to overworking, overeating, overspending, overworrying—anything to prevent you from surrendering to stillness.

The Soul, which is quiet but persistent, requires you to be silent and listen. Only in stillness can you make out its muted whispers.

"The Ego is capable of suspiciousness, at best, and viciousness at worst," warns the *Course*. If you listen to the Ego, *"you'll see yourself as tiny, vulnerable and afraid. You'll experience depression, a sense of worthlessness and feelings of impermanence. You'll believe yourself helpless and the world directs your destiny."*

If you've ever been a victim of abuse, you are especially susceptible to the Ego. The more viciously you were mistreated as a child, or even as an adult, the more tenacious is the Ego, and the more vigilant you must be against it (more about this later).

THE CONFLICTING AGENDAS OF:	
EGO	**SOUL**
Voice of Fear	**Voice of Love**
Source of false power	Source of true power
Its job is to keep you safe	Its job is to make sure you soar
Learned its job in childhood	Gets its marching orders from God
Focuses on your flaws	Reminds you of your gifts
Tells only lies	Speaks only truth
Urges you to hide	Pushes you to shine
Defensive and impatient	Peaceful and accepting
Makes excuses	Takes action
Compares self with others	Has compassion for self and others
Sees only the past	Sees everything as a gift
Craves the comfort of the familiar	Favors the uncertainty of the unknown
Aspires to mediocrity	Aspires to Greatness
Speaks first and loudest	Is quiet but persistent
Depends on busyness and addictions	Requires stillness

Plugging into Your Soul

> *"Love will enter immediately into any mind that truly wants it, but it must want it truly."*
>
> —*A Course in Miracles*

Sacred Success is designed to plug you directly into the hushed, loving voice of your Soul, helping you disregard the Ego's frightful diatribes. The differences can be so subtle, however, that they may be difficult to distinguish and easily misinterpreted. Making the distinction between Ego and Soul is the ongoing challenge of *Sacred Success*. Understanding this polarity, being ever mindful of the disparities, was pivotal for me, as it is for most women who attend my *Sacred Success* retreats.

"It's been major for me," said *Sacred Success* graduate Erin Lewis, twenty-eight, an insurance agent, about trusting her Soul's voice. "It's not as loud, as booming, and as convincing as the Ego's 'car salesman' voice," she explained, "but it is always right. It's like I'm gliding, everything is so easy, so graceful, so simple, the next steps are so obvious. Daring to trust the Soul has been huge for me. That's how I live my life now."

Sensing those discrepancies, no matter how slight they may be, is the secret to sourcing your authentic power.

"When I'm coming from my Soul, I feel more lighthearted, more open, more connected to others and the Universe," declared nutrition store owner Suzy Carroll, forty-eight. "When it's Ego, I'm much more closed down, unreceptive, and in fear. It's like my hands are around a washcloth and I'm squeezing it. That's how I feel internally. I feel tense. My energy feels repressed. When I'm feeling that way, I know that I need to shift gears."

In *Sacred Success*, we learn to shift gears through an endless series of conscious decisions to feed the Soul and starve the Ego. *"Any attempt to master fear is useless,"* the *Course* reminds us. *"The true resolution lies entirely on mastery through love."*

As I have come to see, exercising true power is, in effect, an expression of love. Otherwise, we're conning ourselves (and alienating others) by employing cheap power, using anger, manipulation, control to get our own way. It's the difference between domination and dominion, between the traditional model and the emerging paradigm.

Heroine's Journey

"You have been thinking one way. Now you have to think a different way."

—Joseph Campbell

"Women have long been estranged from their power," Native American shaman Starhawk points out. "Reclaiming our personal power is a healing journey. We have to do battle with our own thought forms."

Sacred Success, at its core, is a healing journey. The battle is always between listening to our Ego or our Soul, choosing between fear and love.

In my book *Prince Charming Isn't Coming*, I likened the process of financial independence to a Hero's Journey, and often quoted the late mythologist Joseph Campbell, who explained that the purpose of all Heroes' Journeys is the "transformation of consciousness," releasing the old, receiving the new.

However, as I have since discovered, the way Heroines often begin their journeys and what they gain from them is significantly different. In traditional accounts, the male Hero, responding to "The Call" (something's missing or was taken), sets out in search of treasure (a helpless maiden or priceless artifact), traveling into the wilderness (out of his comfort zone), confronting monsters/dragons/ordeals (his fears), and ultimately finding treasure (something *outside* of himself). In the traditional Hero's Journey, the woman's role is the passive princess.

The Heroine's Journey also begins with "The Call" (the subject of the next chapter). Unfortunately, women frequently respond differently than their male counterparts, by reverting to tradition—waiting to be saved. Thus there are two kinds of Heroines: those who undertake the journey through their own volition and those who are forced by a crisis. One of my purposes, in writing this book, is to persuade you to partake voluntarily, not procrastinate until disaster strikes.

Just like the guys, Heroines then travel into the wilderness (their discomfort zone) where they also battle dragons and experience ordeals (our Egos personified) before returning to safety. "All this dragon killing has to do with getting past being stuck," says Campbell. We slay the dragons by letting go of limiting beliefs, parental messages, all the stories we tell ourselves, or as Campbell says, "throwing off the old and coming into the new."

Ultimately, Heroines, too, reach the treasure, but it's neither a handsome prince nor anything external. The treasure is a piece of herself she had lost—her power. And retrieving her power is precisely what saves her.

Breaking Rules

"If you obey all the rules you miss all the fun."

—*Katharine Hepburn*

Joseph Campbell observed that often the journey begins with defiance: The Heroine does something she's not supposed to do.

"Life really begins with the act of disobedience," he told Bill Moyers during a PBS special interview, using the example of Adam and Eve. "Now God must've known very well that man was going to eat the forbidden fruit," Campbell said. "But it was by doing this that man became the initiator of his own life."

Originally, I thought our forbidden fruit was money. But now I see clearly that our *real* forbidden fruit is power. To become initiators of our own lives, we must disobey the Ego's warnings and stay mindful of our Soul's gentle guidance. It requires courage to challenge taboos, battle our fears, feel foreboding, and keep on going. The opposite of courage is not fear, but automatic conformity.

Sacred Success is about systemic change, which mandates bucking tradition, breaking old rules—rules made by the patriarchy to keep women in their place, to keep society functioning in a predictable manner, as well as the rules created by the Ego to ensure your survival in your family system.

Rules are important. They create order, stability, and safety. All of us live by rules, personal and societal. Some of them are obvious. Others may be unconscious. As children, we discovered our limits by testing the rules. And we all know what happened when we broke the rules. We got punished. So it makes sense that the mere thought of disobedience almost *always* arouses fear and resistance. Our knee-jerk response is self-protection (the Ego doing its job). Self-protection, however, is only beneficial when there's an actual threat to our existence—otherwise, self-protection becomes an act of self-sabotage, a means of playing small. As my favorite bumper sticker points out, "Obedient women seldom make history."

The key here is to distinguish between what is truly a personal danger and what is actually a healthy sign of growth. The Ego sees growth as a threat. The Soul knows growth is the path to power. So I ask you, as we embark on our journey: What are the rules you've been living by? Which ones serve you? Which ones don't? Which of those rules do you know, or suspect, need breaking?

To help you identify rules that have been governing your life, but are no longer beneficial, here are our first two exercises.

EXERCISE: Revealing Your Rules

Finish each sentence with the first word or words that come to mind. Don't try to find the "perfect" word or think too much about what to say. Go with your gut reaction. As with all the exercises throughout this book, what's important is not necessarily what you write initially, but what the exercise triggers later on, while you're driving to work, taking a shower, or falling asleep.

1. If you asked my father about me achieving Greatness, he'd say

2. If you asked my mother about me achieving Greatness, she'd say

3. If I achieve Greatness, I worry I will

4. I want to achieve Greatness, but

5. To me, achieving Greatness means I have to

6. What terrifies me about achieving Greatness is

7. What excites me about achieving Greatness is

8. In my family, I wasn't supposed to

9. I'd say that my forbidden fruit is

10. Growing up, I knew better than to

11. As a kid, I'd get punished if I

12. Even now, I know I shouldn't

13. My biggest fear of success is

14. If I got too "big," I would

What did you discover in completing each sentence?

EXERCISE: Exploring Your Challenges

Look at all the challenges, obstacles, fears, pains, frustrations, upsets, and troubles that are in your life right now. Write them down. Do you see a theme? Do they reflect any rules that may need breaking?

The Four Stages of *Sacred Success*

> *"To change is to attain a state unlike the one in which you found yourself before."*
>
> —*A Course in Miracles*.

Reclaiming your power often requires a dramatic shift in your state of mind, potentially reversing generations of cultural conditioning and a lifetime of personal programming. That's what the transformational process of *Sacred Success* is designed to help you do. The process consists of the *Outer Work* (practical), *Inner Work* (psychological), and *Higher Work of Wealth* (spiritual). The power is *derived from* the process itself. If you try to shortcut the process, you'll short-circuit your power.

The process is comprised of four stages, each undertaken in specific steps. Because it is Soul-directed, the beauty of *Sacred Success* is that the stages unfold naturally. No exertion is necessary, only mindfulness. Your job is to tune into your Soul's lead, ignoring the Ego's demands as best you can. There's no need to strain or strive to enter a particular stage. Your role is simply to commit to the process, recognize the stages, and do what's necessary in each stage.

The four stages, which we will explore in the following chapters, are:

Stage 1—The Call to Greatness (Chapter 3)

Stage 2—Receptive Surrender (Chapter 4)

Stage 3—Disciplined Action (Chapters 5 and 6)

Stage 4—Modeling Greatness (Chapter 7)

This process isn't necessarily linear. *Sacred Success* is more like a subtle dance—a tango of sorts—that begins with the discomfort of the Call, then steps back into Receptive Surrender, moving forward with Disciplined Action, stepping back when cued by the Call, stepping ahead when ready to act, repeating the steps over and over.

Granted, the dance's subtleties can be easy to miss. Especially for hesitant Heroines. Sometimes it takes a big bang, like a job loss or health scare, to get our attention. In *Sacred Success*, however, we recognize disappointment, even disaster, for what it really is—not just a problem to solve, but the path to a solution. Rather than curse the pain, we look for the lesson it has to teach us.

We begin our Rite of Passage with the following realization: *Where you are right now in your life, whatever is going on, is perfect. Where and how far you go next depends on how much you're willing to release and what you're willing to receive.*

CHAPTER SUMMARY: Preparing for the Passage

- The more you're willing to release your beliefs and assumptions, the greater are your chances of achieving Greatness and your utmost prosperity.
- *Sacred Success* is both a practical process and a spiritual practice, equally sacred and mundane, divinely guided while grounded in action.
- The Four Core Principles of Wealth and Power:
  1. Financial well-being is essential to achieving Greatness.
  2. Our financial foundation is only as strong as our individual integrity.
  3. Power demands responsibility.
  4. Our power comes from one of two sources—Love or Fear.
- The Soul is the voice of Love, or true power. The Ego is the voice of Fear, or false power.
- The Ego aspires to mediocrity; the Soul, to Greatness. Where you head depends on whose voice you heed.
- *Sacred Success* is designed to plug you directly into the hushed, loving voice of your Soul, helping you disregard the Ego's frightening attacks.
- Making the distinction between Ego and Soul is the ongoing challenge of *Sacred Success.*
- *Sacred Success* is a Heroine's Journey, a Rite of Passage into our power.
- *Sacred Success* demands bucking tradition, breaking old rules, which usually arouses fear and resistance.
- Our knee-jerk response is self-protection (the Ego doing its job).
- The trick is to distinguish between what is truly a personal danger and what is actually a healthy sign of growth.
- *Sacred Success* is a transformational process that combines the *Outer Work* (practical), *Inner Work* (psychological), and *Higher Work of Wealth* (spiritual).
- The process is comprised of four stages:
  - Stage 1—The Call to Greatness
  - Stage 2—Receptive Surrender

- ○ Stage 3—Disciplined Action
- ○ Stage 4—Modeling Greatness
- We begin this Rite of Passage with the following realization: *Where you are right now in your life, whatever is going on, is perfect. Where and how far you go next depends on how much you're willing to release and what you're willing to receive.*

SACRED SUCCESS QUIZ: Are You Ready to Play the New Game of Money?

Before you begin your passage to power, take this quiz to help you determine where you are now.

Read each statement and rate it 1 (doesn't fit), 2 (sometimes fits), or 3 (yep, that's me!)

1. Money is mostly a source of pleasure, not pain or stress.   ____

2. I have ample cash savings.   ____

3. I understand my investments.   ____

4. I welcome opportunities to be uncomfortable.   ____

5. I am conscious of my spending.   ____

6. I have no credit card debt.   ____

7. I never spend more money than I have.   ____

8. I know my worth and ask for it.   ____

9. I am committed to not just safeguarding but growing my money.   ____

10. I support causes I'm passionate about.   ____

11. I consider the money I have as mine (even if partnered, I have money in my own name).   ____

12. I really love and appreciate money.   ____

13. I admire most people who have money.   ____

14. I participate fully in financial decisions.   ____

15. I desire to use my money for a cause I feel passionate about.   ____

16. I feel confident about my ability to manage money.   ____

17. I enjoy talking/reading about finances.   ____

18. I have big dreams, convinced I can achieve them.   ____

19. I enjoy downtime, relaxing, with nothing to do.   ____

Total Score: ____

If your total score is . . .

57–47

You've got what it takes to play *Sacred Success*. In fact, chances are, you're already in the game. Use this book to locate any blocks or to identify tips for achieving even more Greatness.

46–35

You've got some brushing up to do, but you're ready to play. Use this book to strengthen your weak links, the items you scored 1 or 2. With a few tweaks, Greatness can be yours.

34 or less

You've still got a lot of work, but what better time to do it! Use this book to transform your thinking and your behavior, so when you turn the last page, you are right on target for achieving Greatness.

PART TWO

The Process

CHAPTER 3

The Call to Greatness—Stage 1

"Be not content with littleness . . . only in magnitude, which is your home . . . You do not have to strive for it because you already have it. All striving must be directed against littleness."

—A Course in Miracles

Where It All Started . . .

"What if your hunger is holy?"

—LiYana Silver

I vividly remember waking up on the first morning of my four-day getaway, which my business coach had strongly recommended. It was late July 2009. I'd needed a break. I'd been feverishly but futilely chasing an ambitious goal: *Make millions, help millions, give millions,* which was to be the subject of my next book. Now, three years and dozens of interviews later, the book remained unwritten, my goal unmet. I'd spent my entire career helping women achieve financial success, yet I was nowhere near my seven-figure goal. In fact, this had been my least profitable year in ages. And I hadn't a clue why or what to do about it.

I lay in bed for a while, sinking deeper into self-pity, until I forced myself to get up. Midway to the bathroom, I stopped dead in my tracks. Suddenly, out of nowhere, I heard a distinct voice in my head say, with commanding authority, "Go for Greatness."

Those three words struck me with the force of a lightning bolt. They came from somewhere very deep, from something very wise. Greatness was not a term I'd often used before. I ran back to bed, grabbed my journal from the nightstand, and started writing.

"Isn't that what I really want, Greatness?" The words flowed quickly, mindlessly, automatically. "I've been so focused on achieving fame and fortune, making millions, helping millions, but those are goals from my Ego. My Soul has been yearning for something very different. It wants Greatness."

It never had occurred to me, until that moment, that there was a distinction. I continued writing. "Making millions seemed the obvious next step. It felt impressive—it certainly was feeding my Ego. What I didn't realize—my Soul was starving."

Pausing to digest this new insight, I was struck by a metaphor that perfectly described my present predicament: "Seeking fame and fortune is the quest for external validation to fill an internal void. It's like living on credit—a pretense, an illusion hiding lack and deprivation. Greatness, on the other hand, is the pursuit of meaning and impact, living life to the fullest while leaving a legacy for the world."

It was a eureka moment! All those feelings I'd been struggling with—burnout, self-pity, frustration—were actually signs that my Soul was calling me to Greatness.

I'd been seeking fame and fortune to justify my worth. But what I truly coveted were opportunities to fulfill my purpose, live my truth, and make an impact. I still wanted to earn more. But millions was no longer what I craved. I could almost hear my Soul sigh with relief.

I spent the rest of the day reviewing the transcripts of my interviews with women who made millions. This time, I read them with a fresh perspective, thanks to my new understanding. Sure enough, I saw something I'd completely missed. Each woman had indeed received the Call to Greatness, but it wasn't until much later, if at all, that she understood what it meant. One entrepreneur actually told me, "Pain is a catalyst to find your Soul." (Fascinating that I never noticed that quote until I reread the interview during this time-out.)

The Call is your Soul summoning you to a higher level, a new phase, your next chapter. It's an invitation, or, more precisely, a command, with an urgent message—something needs to change; there *is* another way and you can, you *need*, to find it. Here's what I wrote in my journal that first morning of my retreat. It felt like I was taking dictation directly from my Soul:

> *Stop what you're doing. Pay attention. It's time to play a bigger game. It's time to own your power and honor your value, not in false arrogance or feigned confidence, but in humble acceptance that you are on this planet for a purpose, and that you have everything needed to fulfill it. It's time to find and fulfill your purpose with confidence and gratitude for the grace and the gifts bestowed upon you, knowing you're here to do God's work.*

When Bigger Is Beckoning

> *"Readiness is the only prerequisite for accomplishment."*
>
> —A Course in Miracles

I am convinced that women all over the world are receiving the Call. But few respond. Most, like me, misinterpret the signs or ignore them completely. Perhaps you're one of them. If you want to know what the signs are, ask yourself this question: Why did I choose this book? I suspect that the reason you're reading *Sacred Success* is because you too have heard the Call. Perhaps you've been feeling discontented, restless,

anxious, unfulfilled, frustrated, bored, or burned out. These are all signs
that Greatness is calling you.

When I asked women what brought them to my *Sacred Success*
retreats, each described similar feelings. "I was trying to write music,
but I had no creative ideas," Luci Butler, a young aspiring songwriter,
complained. "I thought it meant I wasn't capable, and yet this crazy
music writing kept coming back to me in all these weird and magical
ways, making me want to do it so badly."

Others like Karin, a middle-aged director of a nonprofit, simply
sensed, "There's got to be more to life than this." She was having "a lot of
problems in my relationship. I had written a book but wasn't marketing
it. There was more I wanted to do in the world. But what?"

For some, the Call was confusing and guilt-inducing because their
lives were so good they couldn't understand why they felt bad. I think of
Erin Lewis, a spunky twenty-eight-year-old who owned a thriving insurance company, in love with a man she would later marry. Even though
her firm ranked in the top 25 percent of her region, and her relationship
was "amazing," she admitted, "I was going through the motions day in,
day out, not really inspired. I was bored. I was looking for more."

A few were reluctant to even admit something was askew. Cyndy
Bragg, a former TV producer, was an energetic suburban housewife
with a terrific sense of humor. She appeared quite happy, grateful that
her husband's success allowed her to stay home with her kids, "washing more sippy cups than should be humanly allowed." But her bubbly
facade began showing cracks. "During the retreat, I was finally honest
about my frustration," she admitted. "I was mourning the loss of my
six-figure career. I had moved from New York City to a small town in
Maryland. I really wanted to go back to work, but I also wanted to stay
home with my kids. I was confused and lost."

Her candid admission unlocked an array of concealed possibilities. "Honesty allowed me to think and dream and focus on 'what if,'"
Cyndy later told me. "You taught me how to listen to my Soul, to find

my purpose, and I discovered a grander version of myself. As a result my life has shifted dramatically. Now I'm living authentically."

Cyndy discovered her gift as stand-up comedian. These days, while still home with her kids, she's performing at comedy clubs, appearing regularly on local television, and pursuing her certificate in applied positive psychology ("to become a positive psycho," she said with a laugh).

The key to navigating *Sacred Success* with ease, grace, and finesse is paying close attention to the emotional subtleties, the quiet whispers, the tender tickles, the smallest discomforts, admitting, at least to yourself, what's no longer working.

When you ignore these proddings, you do so at your peril. The faint whispers will make themselves heard, often in the form of a painful crisis or loss. For Victoria Trabosh, forty-three, an executive coach making "a good six figures," her Call came in the form of mounting debt, which was taking a big toll on an otherwise very successful career.

"You truly have no idea how blocked, confused, burned out I was when I came to the retreat," she recalled. "I love coaching. I'm very good at it. I know how to make money. But," she confessed, "I don't manage it."

For Victoria, "Money was attached to shame, and heartache, and difficulty." This awareness—that her debt kept her "playing small," was her first step toward eventual solvency and an improved quality of life.

Some women came to my retreats feeling as if their lives were falling apart. And, for Molly, fifty-one, an attorney on the brink of divorce, her life was truly in shambles. "I was in a very bad place. I didn't want to practice law anymore. I had no direction. After eighteen years of marriage, I was lost."

Whatever form the Call takes, it always involves some degree of discomfort. The discomfort—be it mild or intense—is a warning light indicating it's time to course-correct. The status quo is fraying, the old ways aren't working, you need to do things differently. Release what no longer serves you. Pursue what you truly desire. The Call is your

Soul nodding its head in assurance, letting you know that there *really is* another way.

By the end of that first day of my new awareness, I understood why I'd felt so out of sorts, and I got very excited about going for Greatness.

What Is Greatness?

> *"It's not enough to be very good if you have the ability to be great."*
>
> —*Alberta Lee Cox*

Day two of my hiatus had turned cold and grey, not unusual for a Northwest summer. I curled up under a blanket on the window seat in my room, supported by large cushy pillows, staring at the water, pondering Greatness.

I liked the sound of the word. But to tell the truth, I was also intimidated by it. I consulted *Merriam-Webster* online, which told me "Greatness" describes someone who is "remarkable in magnitude, degree, or effectiveness." I thought of women I consider models of Greatness: Mother Teresa, Eleanor Roosevelt, Meryl Streep, Oprah Winfrey.

But I also thought of my daughters—one an organic farmer, another a nursery-school teacher turned jewelry designer, and the oldest, a writer and stay-at-home mom. I may be biased, but I honestly see my girls going for Greatness, each in her own way.

While surfing the internet, seeking guidance for my dilemma, I chanced upon a quote by Fred Buechner: "*The place where God calls you is the place where your deep gladness and the world's deep hunger meet.*" Bingo! I exclaimed to myself. That's what Greatness really means. It's the place where God (your Soul) is summoning you to go, that intersection where what you love doing meets up with what another person truly needs. (Not to be confused with "Grandiosity," which is the Ego's attempt to conceal its despair by amplifying its superiority.)

"I've always believed in greatness for myself, but I always had a small 'g' in great. I thought the only big 'G' here is God's big 'G,'" Victoria, the executive coach, explained after I shared that quote in our retreat.

"But as you talked about Greatness," she continued, "I had a paradigm shift. I realized I needed to step into my Greatness with a capital 'G.' That's the Greatness God intended for me, not only for myself but for others." Victoria's revelation captured the very essence of Greatness. When you go for Greatness, everyone gains.

I thought of my father, Richard Bloch. He achieved Greatness, not because he founded a major corporation, but because he made it possible for millions of people to have professional tax preparation done at a fraction of the cost CPA firms were charging. And he was doing what he enjoyed most: playing with numbers, solving mathematical puzzles, helping people save money.

I believe every one of us is capable of Greatness. We just need to understand what that word means to us personally. I think back to one retreat, when Luci, the hopeful songwriter who played keyboard with the rock band Trans-Siberian Orchestra, struggled with the term. "I can't distinguish between Greatness and selfish indulgence. I mean, being a rock star is not practical. It doesn't really help anybody out. I thought what I was doing was selfish."

Greatness is far from selfish. Greatness simply means living your truth, sharing your gifts. It's being who you are, which Joseph Campbell once described as: "The privilege of a lifetime!" I believe Greatness is both a privilege *and a duty*. The *Course* even warns us to *"not be content with anything less than Greatness."* The world desperately needs more women—like you—to own their Greatness.

"The call and need of a new era is for Greatness," writes Stephen Covey in *The 8th Habit*. "Find your voice and inspire others to find theirs."

We don't need to be or do anything remarkable or extraordinary. We just need to pay attention to our Soul calling us to live authentically. But be forewarned. Greatness takes guts. No doubt about it.

When Terror Strikes

*"We turn to God when our foundations are being
shaken, only to find it is God who is shaking them."*

—*Anonymous*

Sure, Shakespeare implored us: "Be not afraid of Greatness." But there I was, on day three of my hiatus, filled with anxiety. From the moment I opened my eyes, fear wrapped around me like a second skin, seeping into every pore.

"Why am I so scared?" I wondered. I'd spent the last few days splashing around in the excitement of new discoveries. Now, suddenly, I was waking up drowning in anxiety. A split second later, it made perfect sense.

The Call was beckoning me to play a bigger game, which meant, as I wrote in my journal, "I have to come out of hiding, own my value, honor my wisdom, and express my truth, unequivocally. Greatness demands taking up space, playing full out with everything I've got. Every time I hold back, it's a signal I'm settling for mediocrity and smallness. That's not what I'm on this planet for. It's definitely not what I want to teach others."

Many of the women I had spoken to who made millions told me they experienced the same trepidation. "It's scary to truly shine, to find your Greatness. You have to be so clear who you are," admitted a successful high earner.

When your goal is Greatness, there's no room for hiding or withholding, which is exactly what I'd always done. I thought back to 1989 when I first started my journalism career, penning a weekly column for the *San Francisco Business Times*, eventually syndicating it to over thirty newspapers. My goal was to covertly infuse my pieces with spiritual principles inspired by *A Course in Miracles*. I was quite proud of how I snuck metaphysics into my articles about the workplace, without anyone who wasn't spiritual ever noticing. I did the same in my subsequent books. I've always couched my unconventional views in acceptable verbiage.

But now I saw my antics in a whole new light. I had concealed my truth because I was torn by conflicting goals. A big part of me wanted everyone's approval. That was my Ego, of course. Another part, my Soul, yearned to write candidly without censure. I considered the two mutually exclusive. I ended up censoring myself, dipping my toes in the waters of transparency while still playing it safe, restraining myself for fear of exposure, ridicule, and rejection.

I remembered a line I once read by author Susan Jeffers: "Remove those 'I want you to like me' stickers from your forehead and, instead, place them where they truly will do the most good—on your mirror!" That's exactly what I needed to do.

I took my journal and wrote: "Greatness demands I show up completely, owning my spiritual depth, my brilliance, my expertise."

The instant I scribbled that sentence, my stomach did a belly flop. "Is everyone going to think I'm arrogant?" A big fear of mine! "Or even worse, will the world finally see I'm really just faking it? My brilliance is bullshit; my talents are below average."

"No wonder I'm so scared," I thought, as it gradually dawned on me what was actually happening. My trusty Ego, terrified of Greatness, was already arming itself against criticism, doing its job to shield me from harm. Remember, the Ego learned its role when our survival depended on our parents' approval. Over time, our Ego's lessons became rigid rules to be strictly obeyed, never broken.

To this end, the Call makes a very specific, nonnegotiable demand. You must commit an Act of Disobedience—an essential part of our Heroine's Journey—by breaking the Ego's rules, defying its authority, adhering instead to your Soul's directions.

"If I'd observed all the rules," Marilyn Monroe once declared, "I'd never have got anywhere." Women in my *Sacred Success* retreats eventually come to the same conclusion. "I'm slowly kicking my beliefs one by one to the curb," declared an overworked and underpaid graduate. "These are the things I took on as a child to survive and feel safe. I realize that they have not worked in quite some time and they have kept me on that perpetual hamster wheel."

Another participant, a management consultant, exclaimed in a very soft voice, "I learned that my next frontier for Greatness is to be seen! That to live my purpose, I must be the leader I was born to be, knowing that I have nothing to hide, and that my visibility will serve thousands." This was difficult for her, because, growing up, she was severely punished for speaking up, or as her family called it, "making a scene." She readily admitted, "Visibility scares me to death."

In *Sacred Success*, being scared to death is usually a positive sign. In most cases, fear simply means you're defying your Ego by leaving your comfort zone, an act your Soul knows leads straight to Greatness.

The Ego, hell-bent on sticking to the familiar and conventional, will do everything in its power to prevent you from stepping into (gasp!) the unknown. Going for Greatness—venturing beyond the boundaries of what is safe and known, defying the Ego's prohibitions, feeling the angst yet staying the course—takes courage. Courage is not the absence of fear, but the willingness to act despite your fear.

On that third day, holed up in my hotel room, I made a decision. *This is a risk I'm willing to take.* I'm going for Greatness, and taking every woman I possibly can with me. Because you're still reading, I assume that's the decision you're leaning toward too. It's a decision every woman on this path will *repeatedly* have to make.

"Stepping into my Greatness has been a challenge and very scary at times," said Melanie Ericksen, a successful Florida-based energy healer. "Every time I took a leap—such as raising my rates or shifting my practice out of New York—I moved through my fear and the results were magnificent! More joy, abundance, confidence, and a deep knowing that I am on the right path!"

When we last spoke, Melanie was poised to take another leap: She was about to hold her first seminar. For over twenty-five years, she'd worked exclusively with individuals. After the *Sacred Success* retreat, however, she knew she was being called to teach larger audiences. "It has taken a lot of courage, but I am determined!" she told me a week before her seminar.

That's exactly how you respond to the Call, with courage and determination. First come the signs, be they minor or major, signaling that your Soul is requesting your attention. Next, you acknowledge that you're in the first stage of *Sacred Success*. Finally, you respond to the Call by following four steps.

Responding to the Call in Four Simple Steps

"The only thing standing between me and Greatness is me."

—Woody Allen

When the Call comes, you have two choices: avoidance or action. Avoidance offers temporary relief. But sooner or later, your Soul will revolt until you give in. Where do you start? Step 1. As you'll learn, all the stages begin with a question.

STEP 1. ASK YOURSELF: WHAT DO I *REALLY* WANT?

"Desire is the starting point of all achievement."

—Napoleon Hill

This critical question came to me on the fourth and final day of my hiatus, from the same voice that, three days prior, had urged me to go for Greatness. This time, the question was posed with a fierce sense of urgency, as if I had to figure out the answer before I'd ever find Greatness. I know now that's exactly what I needed to do.

I took time to mull over this question, journaling, meditating, searching my Soul while tuning out, as best I could, my Ego's repudiation. I needed to be clear about what *I* wanted. Not what my partner, my parents, or even my publisher wanted. What do *I* want? I call this the "Power Question." We can never fully reclaim our power without a clear answer here.

As I learned long ago, we stop being a victim the moment we take responsibility. And responsibility, in the context of *Sacred Success*, is the ability to respond in healthy ways, (as opposed to using manipulation or control) to get what you *REALLY* want.

According to the *Course*'s wisdom, "*What else could I desire but the truth about myself?*" Yet—what do *I* want?—is not a question many women, or men for that matter, ask themselves. Nor is it easy to answer. As humorist and writer Mark Twain once quipped: "I can teach anybody how to get what they want out of life. The problem is that I can't find anybody who can tell me what they want."

The *Course* counsels us, "*In any situation in which you are uncertain, the first thing to consider is 'what do I want to come of this.'*" Clarification determines the outcome: "*You will make every effort to overlook what interferes with the accomplishment of your objective and concentrate on everything that helps you meet it.*"

I begin each of my retreats with an exercise. I ask every attendee to write down what they want to happen in this retreat or *as a result of* this retreat. I ask you the same question. What do you want to happen *as a result of* reading this book?

EXERCISE: What Do I Want as a Result of Reading *Sacred Success*?

Write down your response in this box.

I recently received an email from a woman who had attended a workshop of mine years earlier. "At some point in my youth," she wrote,

"I stopped asking for things that I wanted because the answer was always 'No.' Now that I am well into my thirties, I realize that I have been so used to assuming that the answer will be 'No,' that not only do I not ask for what I want, I don't even *know* what I want. Do you have any tricks up your sleeve that could help me uncover what I want?"

At the end of this chapter are several "tricks," or exercises, for figuring out what you want. However, a good place to start is simply by making a list. I began with the obvious: good health, happy marriage, financial security. Then I went deeper: I want to make Soul-centered choices, not Ego-driven ones. I want more time for deep connection with God, myself, and those I love. I want the courage to write transparently, authentically. I want more opportunities for leadership and creative expression.

Before my four-day break, my list would've been very different, with words like "fame," "recognition," and "praise." But now I realized I couldn't possibly step into my Greatness if I needed everyone's approval. This discovery is vital to *Sacred Success* and perhaps, as women, our greatest challenge. I witness how often women I work with confront this very issue.

As soon as she returned from her first *Sacred Success* retreat, Canadian Charlene White, the vice president of finance for an international firm, began having problems with her boyfriend. "He was uncomfortable with my power, and attempted to diminish me," she said. But instead of watering herself down, she stood her ground firmly. "I can't be everything to everybody and still own my value and stand in my Greatness!" she declared adamantly. "He will accept it, or not. Just as we lovingly, enthusiastically, cheer on a toddler who unsteadily takes her first steps—we don't berate and yell at her when she falls—so must I treat myself with that same loving kindness as I learn to take my first steps to Greatness."

When the relationship ended, Charlene was heartbroken, but unwavering. "I cannot, I will not, be less than who I am for anybody," she said firmly. "Amen, sister," I thought. This is exactly what a powerful woman sounds like. I've since embraced her words as the rallying cry of *Sacred Success*: *I cannot, I will not, be less than who I am for anybody.*

STEP 2: UNDERSTAND THE LAW OF ATTRACTION AND THE LAW OF CONGRUENCY.

"Whatever you accept into your mind has reality for you. It is your acceptance of it that makes it real."

—A Course in Miracles

As you gain a clearer sense of what you want and don't want, your next step is to go even deeper by understanding the Law of Attraction, which states that *you attract whatever you want into your life through your ability to feel good, think positively, and focus only on the desired outcome.*

This law is a favorite among New Age seekers, made popular by the book and movie *The Secret.* However, there is a little-known catch to this law that can get you into trouble. It has to do with what I've labeled the Law of Congruency, which goes like this: *You get what you want, not what you ask for.* Congruency, which is a sign of integrity, means your declared intention must be consistent with your unconscious decisions.

For example, you may say "I want to be rich," but if, deep down, you distrust wealthy people, don't believe you deserve more, or consider money the root of all evil, then wealth isn't *really* what you want.

"What you ask for, you receive," the *Course* explains. *"But this refers to prayers of the heart, not the words you use in praying."*

In my case, I was claiming I wanted to make millions, but deep down, what I truly longed for was authentic expression. This inner discord explains why affirmations, visualizations, or positive thinking, as powerful as they are, don't always work—your spoken goals may be in direct conflict with your genuine desires. Unconsciously, you don't actually want what you've been asking for.

How do you know what you want? Look at what you've got. As the *Course* explains, you are answering this question *"every minute and every second."* If you don't like what you see, ask yourself this question: If I don't have what I desire, why don't I want it? Believe me, there's a part of you, the Ego, of course, that mistakenly views your desires as a threat to its existence. But the Soul, as your unswerving connection with the Source, knows you *are* safe and wants you to shine doing what you were born to do.

EXERCISE: Asking the Ego

Ask yourself this question, knowing the Ego will readily respond: *If I don't have what I desire, why don't I want it?* Write down, in the space below, whatever comes to mind.

STEP 3: FIGURE OUT WHERE YOU'RE GIVING YOUR POWER AWAY.

"If you don't like being a doormat then get off the floor."

—Al-Anon

How do you know where you're giving your power away? Look at where you're not happy. Consider the people, things, emotions, circumstances, or anything that seems to "make you" unhappy. You may also notice that every time you relinquish your power, you are disregarding one or more of the Four Core Principles—by being financially irresponsible, showing a lack of integrity, laying blame, or listening to Ego.

I started a list in my journal of where or to whom I was giving my power away and kept adding to the list long after my return home. My list included the economy, my business, other people's approval, the publishing industry, and most of all, I realized, money, or more precisely, making millions. There's nothing wrong with wanting to earn more, but I'd given profit way too much power. Financial gain had become my focal point, my identity, the source of my joy, the cause of my suffering. I was out of integrity, in cahoots with my Ego.

It was time to take that power back. I knew this was the work I needed to be doing when I got home. And indeed it was. I started this process on my four days away by telling myself the truth about why I'd been so frustrated and unhappy, how my lusting after fame and fortune was fear based and Ego driven.

Then I had to feel my anger. Anger is an unavoidable by-product of powerlessness, though often we push it down until it's quietly seething under the surface. I had no trouble finding mine. Mostly I was angry at myself for getting sucked into my Ego's insecurity, for taking so long to realize how far I'd veered off course.

To fully retrieve my power, I had to forgive myself. I did this by admitting the problem, feeling my anger, then finding gratitude. Whatever produces anger also provides many gifts. I realized that my failure to make millions had catapulted me straight into *Sacred Success*, which has significantly changed my life, as well as countless others.

STEP 4. PAY ATTENTION BY OBSERVING YOURSELF.

> *"When you do things from your Soul, you feel a river moving in you, a joy."*
>
> —*Rumi*

You pay attention by simply observing what goes on *around you* and *in you*. Start being a witness to yourself, a neutral spectator, objectively viewing your life without shame, blame, or judgment. Notice when you repeat old patterns, act out false beliefs, or submit to your Ego's fear. Then say to yourself: *Isn't this interesting. Perhaps there's another way to see this. Maybe I can do this differently.*

For example, Noele, a professional volunteer who served on many nonprofit boards, made a "huge Post-it note" of the differences between the Ego and the Soul. "Every day," she told me, "I'd reflect on where I put my power (energy), noticing when I was acting from my Ego's old story. Then I'd consciously rewrite a new script from my Soul's Call to Greatness. This is so much fun and so powerful to check myself and make more positive, great choices."

She even recruited her husband. "I asked him to listen to me talk about something that is going on and tell me which side of the chart I'm talking from. He is quite good at helping me see where I give away my own power to my Ego and where I fuel myself toward Greatness."

This critical skill, paying attention by observing yourself, lies in the realm of the Soul. The Ego always starts with doing, busily plotting lots of activity—pure distraction—a form of self-sabotage.

Entering Stage 2

"As human beings, our greatness lies not so much in being able to remake the world, as in being able to remake ourselves."

—Mahatma Gandhi

As you respond to the Call by asking yourself what you *really* want, practicing the Law of Attraction and the Law of Congruency, contemplating where you're giving your power away, and paying close attention to what goes on internally and externally, you may or may not notice a subtle shift is occurring. Eventually, you'll realize you're in Stage 2.

I came home from my four days away totally on fire, completely revitalized, eager to forge ahead. Naturally, I did what any Energizer Bunny would do—I kept doing what I'd always done, with even more vigor and intensity. The Call grew louder. My computer crashed. My longtime assistant quit. My business slowed to nearly a crawl. I was stymied. All I knew to do was pray (beg, actually) for guidance.

As the leaves began turning colors, my mentor and dear friend, Karen McCall, founder of Financial Recovery Institute, came for a visit and to work on her book. I asked her to help me resuscitate my business. A few days later, she made a startling observation.

"Do you realize how much power you're giving to your business partner?" she said, ticking off all the ways I'd handed Linda control of the company, though she had never explicitly asked for it.

I felt my stomach drop. I'd long suspected, but never admitted, that our partnership wasn't working. We had such different personalities. It was so much easier for me to relinquish control than it was to exert it. I knew I needed to address the matter. Yet I couldn't risk losing Linda. I was convinced there was no way I could run the business on my own, sure my world would fall apart if she left.

But Karen wisely observed: "If it's not working for you, it's not working for her." She was right. I had taken the easy way out for far too long.

After some tough conversations, Linda and I agreed to part ways. By December, our divorce was final. I let Linda go with love. I grieved the loss, took full responsibility for my role in our separation, and sank into a tailspin of worry about my professional future. Less than two weeks later, out of the blue, a major corporation hired me as a spokesperson for a three-city, eight-day tour, a two-hour Twitter campaign, and a slew of media interviews. It was a highly lucrative deal, considerably boosting my bottom line. (Funny how often good fortune strikes as soon as we tell our truth, face our fear, and let go of what's holding us back.)

But between the breakup and the traveling, I was exhausted. As winter approached, I remember saying to my boyfriend, Lee, with a heavy sigh, "I wish I could take a month off."

"Why don't you?" he responded.

"I can't!" I snapped, thinking of all the "important" things I had to do.

But as soon as I said it, I knew I was entering Stage 2.

CHAPTER SUMMARY: The Call to Greatness—Stage 1

- The Call is your Soul summoning you to play a bigger game.

- Signs of the Call include feeling discontented, restless, anxious, unfulfilled, frustrated, bored, or burned out.

- Definition of Greatness—*the place where your deep gladness and the world's deep hunger meet.*

- Greatness takes guts. You must come out of hiding, break the Ego's rules, own the fullness of who you are.

- Fear is a positive sign, indicating you're defying your Ego by doing what you fear. Greatness is always found just beyond your comfort zone.

- You respond to the Call by taking four steps:

  - Step 1: Ask yourself: What do I *really* want?

  - Step 2: Understand the Law of Attraction and the Law of Congruency.

  - Step 3: Figure out where you're giving your power away.

  - Step 4: Pay attention by observing yourself.

STAGE 1 HOMEWORK

Here are two additional exercises that will help you gain clarity, pay attention, and determine what you really want.

EXERCISE: The Do/Be/Have List

Divide your life into these seven categories: Spiritual, Mental, Physical, Vocational, Financial, Family, and Social.

Think about what you want to *do*, *be*, and *have* in each of these seven categories. Start making a list, taking time to flesh out each group. This will take several sittings. Don't stop at the first draft. The idea is to keep digging deeper, to keep uncovering the truth hidden in your heart, and write it down. Don't restrain yourself by trying to be reasonable, practical, or realistic. In fact, err in the direction of fantasy, as if you had a magic wand with no limit on wishes.

Don't be surprised if you resist doing this. I did for a long time, when my coach, Margery Miller, assigned it to me. And so do many of my clients. It's a profoundly effective exercise. As in any endeavor, the amount of resistance you experience is directly linked to the amount of power and pleasure available on the other side. I urge you to give it a go. The results may surprise you.

Spiritual	
Mental	
Physical	
Vocational	
Financial	
Family	
Social	

EXERCISE: Power Review

Divide your age into thirds. Write those age ranges at the top of each column. Then think back to experiences you had in each period when you felt powerful, important, skilled, and capable.

Recall something YOU did that went really well, that you felt very proud of, and that made you very happy—anything from learning to tie your shoes, to winning a sailboat race, to writing a story that made some-one laugh. Try to find at least three experiences within each age group.

Then, alongside each experience, describe in a few sentences what you did, the skill you used, and the interests you displayed. Do you see any patterns? Pay particular attention to what brings you great gladness, all those things you do really well and enjoy doing so much that you sometimes take them for granted.

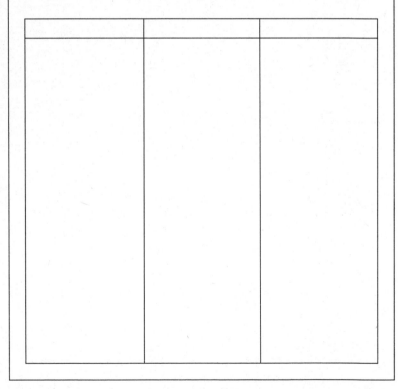

THE SIXTEEN TRAITS OF GREATNESS

Read the following traits of Greatness. Live them, speak them. Put into practice what's meaningful to you. Share what you learn with others.

1. Greatness refuses to be limited or controlled in any way by fear. (Fear is to Greatness what ants are to a picnic—annoying, inevitable, and best ignored.)

2. Greatness follows ideas that seem to come from nowhere.

3. Greatness doesn't act alone. It has partners, collaborators, a team.

4. Greatness is humble, not to be confused with Grandiosity. Grandiosity comes from the Ego and is, as *A Course in Miracles* tells us, "*always a cover for despair.*"

5. Greatness is sourced from the Soul, whose greatest desire is to pursue its purpose.

6. Greatness sees the world as its playground and every problem as part of the Game, where a lawsuit is no more serious than losing a stapler.

7. Greatness takes its mission, not itself, seriously, and always puts that mission first.

8. Greatness truly enjoys Greatness, not just for its own sake, but for its impact on others.

9. Greatness respects and appreciates money. Sufficient income is necessary to eliminate distractions for achieving its goals.

10. Greatness isn't perfect, and is more than willing not to be. Greatness feeds on self-trust (knowing you can clean up what you mess up!).

11. When pain enters Greatness, it's meant to be a wake-up call.

12. Greatness is kind, but tough, and politely endures criticism. While Greatness doesn't need to be liked, it demands to be respected.

13. The arc of Greatness involves many mistakes, failures, wrong turns. Know they are the stepping-stones to Greatness.

14. Greatness is passion made manifest; it is truth unmasked.

15. Greatness requires responsibility, rejects mediocrity, and resides in the unknown.

16. When Greatness dies, it doesn't go away. Greatness always leaves a legacy.

> *"The difference between Greatness and mediocrity is often how one views a mistake."*
>
> —*James Boswell*

CHAPTER 4

Receptive Surrender—Stage 2

"Be willing to surrender what you are for what you could become."

—A Course in Miracles

The Healing Gap

"Take rest; a field that has rested gives a bountiful crop."

—Ovid

My partnership over, I was feeling adrift, unclear about my next steps. But rather than forcing things into focus, I consciously surrendered, allowing the future to unfold at its own pace.

This is not a tack I'd normally take. I'm a go-getter kind of gal. To me, surrender was a pejorative term, something to be avoided by anyone with any ambition. And I was one ambitious woman. Yet as I came to realize, if you don't choose Receptive Surrender, it will choose you.

When I first interviewed women making millions, I was both disturbed and puzzled about why so many suffered a major misfortune just prior to making their fortunes—anything from bankruptcy to breast cancer, from a devastating betrayal to an alcoholic breakdown.

"Is suffering a prerequisite to massive success?" I'd wondered grimly.

However, when I reread the interviews during my four-day hiatus, I began to understand. The Soul will go to great lengths to get our attention. *"Tolerance for pain may be high but it is not without limits,"* warns *A Course in Miracles.*

Those who ignore the Call to Greatness are apt to face a major crisis down the line. Not as punishment or rebuke, but as a wake-up alarm (with no snooze button). Traumas serve as turning points. Many of the women I was interviewing had been left with no choice but to slow down, and in some cases, to stop completely, often spending lengthy periods in the unknown, tolerating (though not enjoying) the uncertainty.

"For months, the only thing I could do was stare out the window and reassess everything," said an investment advisor about her painful bout with meningitis.

"Depression was a gift," said a senior executive. "It forced me to absolutely stop what I'd been doing for eighteen years."

Eventually, as they gave up trying to control their circumstances, allowing things to fall apart without rushing to put them back together, these women realized that these periods of "nothing happening," or as I refer to them, *Points of Pain and Paralysis*, served an essential role in their eventual triumphs.

"I never stopped to figure out who I was. I was told as a kid that I was a loser," said a former alcoholic, referring to her time in rehab as a blessing in disguise. "When I hit bottom, I got sober and I lost my fear. I just knew whatever happened, I'd be okay. I bounced from massive self-doubt to damn-the-torpedo confidence."

We all experience crisis in our lives. But not everyone bounces back from the depths of despair to the summit of success. The secret, for the triumphant ones, was not careful planning, but using time-outs, as one woman put it, "to regroup and come back stronger." They took advantage of what seemed like a limbo to do a lot of soul-searching, self-reflection, and personal development work, dreaming bigger than ever, seizing serendipity whenever it came.

Not one of these women regarded the chaos of uncertainty as an excuse to return to the safety of the known. They correctly sensed that this "in-between" place was a temporary, but compulsory, part of their growth process.

Here's an investment banker, a college dropout, whom I'll call Annie. "One of the most important things I've learned," she told me, "is to just show up and be open to the opportunities that come your way. There was a time when my life was so rush, rush, and frantic, I wasn't enjoying the now." Working as a secretary, cocktail waitress, and aerobics teacher, all at the same time, Annie finally hit bottom. "I was a couple hundred thousand dollars in debt, working three jobs, and I just crashed and burned."

She left the rat race, found a minimum-wage job, and finally surrendered. "I stopped running the show and started listening to myself and going with the synchronicities." As a result, she found a position as a receptionist with an investment banker who taught her the business, and today she runs her own firm, "doing million-dollar deals."

Taking my cue from these women, I decided to take the next month off. I much preferred surrendering by design than default. Little did I realize that what began as a four-week break would turn into a nine-month sabbatical.

I embraced Surrender—or as I referred to it, the Healing Gap—as the precursor to Greatness. I highly recommend you do the same. When the Call comes, voluntarily choose Receptive Surrender by eliminating all but the essentials and creating space for self-reflection. As Picasso is credited with saying, "Without great solitude, no serious work is possible."

I'm not saying it's easy, because it certainly isn't. The Ego will vigorously oppose what it perceives as laziness. But let me explain why downtime is so important.

What? Me, Surrender?!

*"The creative process is a process of surrender, not
control."*

—Julia Cameron

Our frightened Ego, tasked to protect us, needs perpetual motion as
a pretense for control. The Soul, however, as our guide to Greatness,
requires stillness so we can hear the secrets it yearns to share.

There is a Buddhist term that beautifully describes this stage—
Sunyata, which literally means "the value of the void" or "to strive after
the void." Indeed, Receptive Surrender requires that we value the time
between for what it truly is—a primal state of pure energy, the natural
beginning of all creative acts, a fertile field of infinite possibility.

Renowned prosperity author Catherine Ponder explains it this way:
"If you want the greatest prosperity in your life, start forming a vacuum
to receive it."

Surrender is highly underrated in the Western world. Isn't "Sloth"
one of the seven deadliest sins? Society frowns upon fallow time, while
favorably rewarding feverish activity, as if constant motion signifies
actual accomplishment.

However, in the words of Mahatma Gandhi, "Speed is irrelevant if
you're traveling in the wrong direction."

Think of Surrender as a practical strategy to ensure you're proceeding in the direction of Greatness rather than spinning your wheels chasing mediocrity.

I remember reading an interview with George Shultz, former secretary of state, in the *Wall Street Journal*, in which he recalled running
into Steve Jobs' wife at a party. When he asked where her husband was,
she responded: "Oh, Steve's taking six months off to think."

Taking time off was long respected by primitive cultures and East-
ern religions that gave meaning to the void with rites and rituals that

took people from their villages into the wilderness, allowing them to connect with their spirit guides, reassess old ways of being, and contemplate their next phase.

But few in our society teach, or even encourage, this practice anymore. Following these ancient traditions, *Sacred Success* takes us on just such a Rite of Passage into our power. But for most, Surrender feels counterintuitive, more like a waste of time than the way to Greatness. When Erin Lewis, the insurance executive, listened to me describe Surrender at the retreat, her reaction was typical.

"I was like, are you kidding me? My entire life I've always been 'doing.' I've worked since I was fourteen years old," she said, aghast. "The whole concept of getting quiet to listen to your Soul, do nothing, is totally foreign and terrifying to me. I know that came from my mother, who never ever sat still. She was always doing, doing, working, working. There was no time for laziness or sitting."

But as the day progressed, Erin saw the light. Surrender began to make more sense. "I've been extremely successful with lots of structure," Erin mused, "but in order to go to the next level in my career I need to release the structure and allow the Universe to work its mysteries. My Soul craves this right now. If I am going to live my Greatness, I need to change directions, get clear on what I want, go into deep Surrender, and just let the next thing unfold."

She paused, then added, with a look of pure bewilderment, "But I don't know where to start. I mean, what *do* you *do* when you do nothing?"

Good question!

The Beginner's Guide to Surrender

> *"I didn't arrive at my understanding of the fundamental laws of the Universe through my rational mind."*
>
> —Albert Einstein

In one of his poems, Rumi poignantly sums up the art of Receptive Surrender.

> *I said: what about my eyes?*
> *God said: Keep them on the road.*
> *I said: what about my passion?*
> *God said: Keep it burning.*
> *I said: what about my heart?*
> *God said: Tell me what you hold inside it.*
> *I said: pain and sorrow.*
> *He said: stay with it.*
> *The wound is the place where the Light enters you.*

Receptive Surrender is how you allow the healing light to enter your wounded places. You don't need to leave your village, quit your job, or take six months off. Though highly recommended, it's not a realistic option for most people.

The best way to start is by finding patches of stillness in the crazy quilt of your day, clearing your calendar of the nonessential, carving out unstructured time to connect with your Soul. Surrender can be a gradual process, as it was for me. I made it a game. Every morning I asked myself: What can I take off my to-do list today? I eased into it slowly by saying "no" to things that didn't feed my Soul, no matter how lucrative, or tempting. I said "no" to speaking invitations, "no" to networking opportunities, "no" to writing my newsletter and blog. I even turned down a *Family Circle* interview and new coaching clients.

If anyone asked, I was on sabbatical until further notice. As a result I had lots of downtime, which, of course, is the whole point. But to many, downtime is a dirty word. And I know why.

Without endless activity, we're left with empty space. And empty space gives rise to painful feelings. Fear, self-doubt, anger, jealousy, shame—all those vicious demons we've been artfully dodging—will inevitably rear their ugly heads. Rather than experience the pain, we fill up the spaces.

Erin readily agreed. "Busyness is my comfort zone. It's an easy place to be because I don't have to face anything that's scary."

Denial, however, is self-delusion. Demons dodged, emotions repressed, fears not faced will continue to thrive and intensify, sapping our power and producing self-destructive behaviors. But expose them to light, embrace their existence, and inevitably they'll dissipate, losing their potency, if not evaporating entirely.

I once had a business coach, Margery Miller, tell me: "That which we condemn, fear, or resist, we'll breed, attract, and become until we love it." Essentially, our demons are the wounded parts of ourselves longing for love, aching to be heard and healed. As they say in psychotherapy circles—to heal, you must feel.

Eventually, you'll discover, as Tatiana Bredikin, a strategic planner and meeting facilitator, did, "I can experience huge grief and anger and fear, and in the midst of it know that I am choosing to feel the feeling because that is what will move it through me."

Still, I'm the first to admit—busyness is a bitch to give up! Or, as I wrote in a later blog, "Surrender is not for sissies." It's much easier to dive into idle diversions, like shopping online, planning a project, or heeding what my assistant, Lynda Jo Schuessler, refers to as "the siren song of the washing machine."

No Sissies Allowed

"No one achieved Greatness by playing it safe."

—Harry Gray

At first, I was delighted to take a breather. But very quickly, the joy of doing practically nothing faded into frustration and impatience. I

wanted to know my next step, and I wanted it *now*. Surrender, by definition, means relinquishing control, a frightening concept for us control
freaks. I felt like I'd been dropped into a sea of uncertainty, wondering
if I'd ever be productive again, worrying what people must be thinking,
my Ego rebelling. "Do something," it shrieked. "Write a book. Make
more money. You're such a slacker."

I grew angry, irritable, antsy. Try as I might, it was hard to sit still.
I kept getting up, looking for lip balm, sitting down, back up for a bite
to eat, down again, oops, I need a Kleenex, oh my, no Kleenex, off I go
to the store.

I call it *ATBS—Addicted to Busyness Syndrome*. It's epidemic among
women. *Busyness is our drug of choice.* We stuff every cranny of our lives
with so much activity that we've lost touch with what's truly essential
and what's actually irrelevant. We're running around doing what everyone expects—chauffeuring, cleaning, volunteering—convinced that's
our obligation as women.

Yet ask us to lighten our load, actually say no to a task, and we start
to panic as if our world would shatter if we slowed down. The truth is,
we've become so controlled by *shoulds* and *have-tos* that we've lost sight
of what we genuinely value.

Erin, the insurance executive, left the retreat wondering what
new path she should take that truly inspired her. In her quest to
solve this mystery, she confessed, "I was frantic, ferociously trying
to figure it out prematurely because I was so uncomfortable living
in the question."

Instead of sitting in stillness, Erin plunged into self-improvement.
"I spent over $1,000 on three different courses, and hired a coach who
cost me $15,000."

As often happens, Erin went searching "out there" for what can
only be found within. Stephen King said it so well: "It is, after all, the
dab of grit that seeps into an oyster's shell that makes the pearl, not
pearl-making seminars with other oysters."

If we truly aspire to Greatness, we must let the unnerving grit of uncertainty seep into our psyche and give it time to be converted into pearls of wisdom and clarity. Seminars, while often quite helpful, can never substitute for Surrender. Otherwise, personal growth is simply busyness wearing a righteous mask.

"I've spent the last ten years of my life figuring out how to be a better version of me—attending seminars, hiring coaches, reading self-help books," Erin finally realized. "Now, it's time to just live my life as the woman that I've become! Wow. This is a huge transition for me."

Like any drug, busyness is not only a downer, but a dangerous form of self-deception. We fool ourselves into feeling productive, when actually we're impeding our progress. I invite you to start noticing all the needless activities you cram into your life. Then take a few deep breaths and clear your plate as much as possible.

Charlene White, the vice president of finance mentioned earlier, explained it like this, "The distinction for me was that before [the retreat] I'd be still out of exhaustion. Instead of communing with my Soul, I'd be worn out and trying to recover."

To Heal You Must Feel

> *"Repression thus operates to conceal not only the baser impulses, but also the most lofty ones from the ego's awareness, because both are threatening to the ego."*
>
> —A Course in Miracles

There are all sorts of ways to create short intervals of quiet contemplation. Maybe you can't spare a month or even a full day. But what if you didn't load the wash until later in the afternoon? What if you responded to emails only once a day? What if you didn't answer the phone but took it off the hook and just closed your eyes?

Suzy Carroll, who owns a nutrition store, decided to work at home one day a week. "I never would have done that before the retreat," she admitted. "It felt wrong. I needed to be in the store and seen. What are my employees going to think of me? But I've attracted a bunch of wonderful staff people who were very supportive."

She begins her day with meditation. "I call it Take Ten," she explains. "Ten minutes every morning of just quietness. Even on days when I go into the store, those ten minutes start my day out calm and focused. That's when I started creating my Positive Solution Weight Loss Program."

The amount of time spent in Surrender is not as important as how you use the time. The whole point of Receptive Surrender is to finally release what you've been repressing. Being pleasure-seeking creatures, we have a tendency to push down unpleasant emotions, using massive energy to keep them submerged. This "emotional constipation," as one woman referred to it, seriously reduces our power.

Sacred Success, however, asks you to dive into and magnify whatever feelings emerge, allowing those feelings to expand, intensify, escalate. The challenge is to experience them completely, rather than concealing them with extraneous activity or assorted addictions.

As one woman wrote me after the retreat, "The moment I realized it was my childhood fear of feeling different and not being accepted, those old demons didn't seem nearly so threatening."

My biggest fear has always been that I'm not important, I don't matter, and one day, I'll just fade away. This belief—clearly rooted in childhood and utterly irrational—was nonetheless relentlessly brutal, never letting me rest. It didn't matter how many books I wrote or standing ovations I received; I never felt I mattered. Now, without diversions, my fears were amplified.

"It's been horribly uncomfortable not having any drive or focus," I wrote in my journal. "I feel like I'm precariously tipping over the edge of obscurity, like any day, I might disappear."

Making matters even worse, I watched myself slip into compulsive comparing. The more I compared myself with others, the more unimportant I felt and the harder it was to surrender. I felt like a giant "L" (for "Loser") had been tattooed on my forehead for everyone to see. My self-hatred turned into searing pain. "Will it ever go away?" I wondered.

But instead of numbing the pain—having heard the Call to Greatness, knowing I was now in Stage 2 of *Sacred Success*—I found the strength to dive ever deeper. I was determined to discover who I was under that cloak of fear and shame—my own private body armor. I'd spent my whole life trying to hide my unimportance or prove it false, but all I could ever see was evidence of its existence. Psychologists call this confirmation bias, the tendency to confirm our beliefs rather than deny them.

I opened the *Course* and it confirmed that *"Questioning illusions"* (like my *I'm not important*) *"is the first step in undoing them."* And indeed, over time I made a startling realization. I may have dropped off Facebook and Twitter, the speaking circuit and the blogosphere, but I'll be damned, I never *really* disappeared. I was still important to the people who mattered most, like my boyfriend, my kids, my friends, and my family.

As I wrote in *Overcoming Underearning*: "When you learn to face that which makes you fearful, it need never control you again."

My first month of Surrender was drawing to a close. I knew there was no way I was going back to work full-time as I had planned. "I've never felt so unmotivated in my life," I wrote in my journal. "I don't believe my career is over, but I can't see what's next, now that I'm not listening to my Ego. I feel like a boat with no wind in its sails. There's nothing to move me, get me going. It's so weird not being driven by fame and fortune. I'm tired. Depleted. My insides feel bruised from battling for success. I need to rest."

Receptive Surrender takes patience. As one woman put it: "I'm heading straight to Greatness, but at the pace of Surrender." Indeed, Stage 2 progresses at its own tempo, in its own time.

The Payoff

*"I need do nothing. It would be far more profitable
now merely to concentrate on this than consider what
you should do."*

—*A Course in Miracles*

Mindy Goldstein, a senior vice president of a leading financial services firm who described herself as "always running, running, running," knew an extended sabbatical wasn't possible, but Surrender was still important. So evenings and weekends, she'd turn off the TV, take long walks in the park, or simply sit in silence. "I light a candle, close my eyes, go deep into my heart, and use this time for my Soul to speak and my body to share her wisdom," she said. "As I slow down and connect with myself, I feel like I'm taking care of me in a new way."

In the quiet, she allowed her demons of shame and unworthiness to come out of hiding. "I've always known they were there," she said. "But now I'm allowing them to be seen so they can be healed. I want to keep slowing down more and not let distractions get in the way of allowing my feelings to come up."

Not everyone is quite so willing to find time to face her feelings. In fact, most women I work with have all sorts of excuses why it's impractical or impossible. That's often when the Universe intervenes.

Melanie Ericksen, the energy healer we met earlier, intended to significantly reduce her client load, yet couldn't bring herself to do it. Her work was her livelihood. But when she lost her voice for six weeks, she had to cancel all appointments.

"Not being able to talk was like taking my arm away. I felt so vulnerable and frustrated," she said. "And I didn't get better as fast as usual. This scared me and actually slowed me down—I had to go within!"

As she was forced into quiet, things started happening. First the emotions: "I felt cranky, unlovable, and anxious." Next the resistance: "As the fear set in, I'd get busy 'doing.'" Then the insights: "I started seeing all my unhealthy patterns: putting others' needs before mine, saying yes when I wanted to say no, pushing myself nonstop to feel safe, my struggle expressing to the world exactly what I do." Finally, acceptance: "I know that to bring my work fully into the world, I have to keep going deeper into Surrender by doing less. I am surrendering to the fear and replacing it with faith."

Tracey Allred, on the other hand, had way too much time on her hands after she lost her job as a TV producer. She attended the *Sacred Success* retreat to figure out her next career move. When I suggested she spend time in stillness, she grew quite irate.

"I thought this was going to be about money," she snapped in annoyance. "I had no idea that it was going to be about the Ego and Soul. I've been out of work for a while. That's all I've done is be still."

"Were you *really* still?" I asked her.

She paused, then shook her head sheepishly. "Even when I wasn't working I was doing unnecessary stuff, basically to keep me busy, like constantly being at everyone else's beck and call. It's that people-pleasing thing. I was hiding behind a happy mask. But I'd come home and feel like crap. I realize that busyness makes me feel important and gives me a sense of worth."

This recognition hit her hard. Tears welled up. She could barely speak. I watched her struggle to maintain her composure. Sensing that stifling her feelings was her lifelong default mode, I asked her to get up and hit the wall with a towel. Tentatively at first, she began slapping the towel against the wall. As her intensity increased, the tears started flowing. She was breathing hard when she finally sat down.

"I've been stuffing down a lot of emotion," she admitted, as if realizing this for the very first time.

Surrender is challenging for everyone, but for those who've suffered abuse, like Tracey, the experience is exceptionally grueling. Victims of violence have a tenacious Ego that is fiercely resistant to reexperiencing old pain yet at the same time cruelly self-flagellating. Tracey was five years old when the abuse first started.

"I didn't even know until *Sacred Success* that I was in busyness addiction," she said, her voice thick with frustration and fury. "But now I think: Wasn't it just perfect that I was in production where you work twelve, fourteen, twenty hours a day. At first I loved it, but I had no boundaries. By the time I got home I was so exhausted, I fell asleep. I didn't have to feel."

I gave Tracey an assignment that I often give clients. "I want you to write an angry letter to yourself," I told her. "Don't be nice. Let it all out." I thought about having her write to her abusers, but I sensed, as is often the case, the person we're most angry at is actually ourself. Why? We often harbor the false notion that we could have, should have, done more or that we *are* the problem. Underneath the anger lies the painful belief: There's something wrong with *me*.

The next day, she reported back. "When I began writing that letter, I saw how viciously I beat myself up. I didn't realize I was carrying that much hate and anger for myself. I felt such extreme sadness for how I've treated my own self," she said. "I have deep shame that I protected the perpetrators by not speaking up. I didn't want to be the bad girl. I gave away my own voice and my own power and I'm still giving away my power."

But by writing the letter and hitting the wall, she realized, "You've given me healthy ways to express my anger. I felt really rageful, but I also felt a release that I had never felt before."

The release opened her up to a profound realization. "We have emotions for a reason and we need to express them in healthy ways. Holding them down can make you sick." Tracey flashed back to her mother and aunt, both emotionally repressed women who died of cancer at a fairly young age.

In my experience, whatever their history, women in general hold a tremendous amount of unexpressed anger, though few realize it. I've certainly seen it in myself. I see it in just about every woman I coach. Unexpected anger always surfaces at my retreats, to the surprise and sometimes chagrin of many.

"I never saw the purpose of anger for things that I cannot change and that are long over," said Anne de la Guerre, a sweet-faced, easy-going young woman, age thirty-one. "But now I know that it's toxic to let the charge sit inside me. I now see how much rage and shame I've been living with for so long. For me, for the little girl in me, I need to honor the anger and express it. That little girl deserves to have a voice."

Anger is simply energy. Repressed anger immobilizes. Released anger galvanizes. When you discharge your anger, you begin to notice a direct connection between your anger and your power. Suppressing one inhibits expressing the other.

As corporate executive Laura Deveau, age forty-nine, observed, "My power comes from the same place as my anger. So burying my anger can bury my power too." Another woman, a general counsel at an investment bank, realized the same: "When I disconnect from my emotions because I am afraid to feel the pain, I am also cutting myself off from my passion and my power."

EXERCISE: The Angry Letter

If you suspect you, too, may have some buried anger, I invite you to write an angry letter. Write it to another person, your parents or ex-husband, perhaps. Then write one to yourself. Write it by hand, not on a computer. Start the letter with "Dear XX, I am so pissed at you . . ." (using whatever words feel right).

Even if you don't feel any irritation initially, start listing what you *might* be annoyed at. Let yourself get into it. Liberate your fury, your rage, your frustrations. Write until you're done. Fold up the letter and put it away for *no more than three days*.

Then take it out and reread it. Is there anything you want to add? If so, write some more. Continue the process until you feel complete.

When you're finished, burn the letter. As you watch it burn, let your anger go with love. Say to your anger: "Thank you. You served me once. I no longer need you. Now I release you. I am free."

You'll know you've truly released your anger when you can follow it up with a letter of forgiveness, which I suggest you write to complete the process.

What if you've done anger releasing exercises ad nauseam, and damn it, you're still angry? Ask yourself: *What is my payoff for holding on to anger?* Why *don't* I want to let it go? Believe me, the anger is giving you something. Often it's a false or cheap sense of power, invulnerability, and autonomy.

Tracey left the retreat so committed to healing herself emotionally that instead of running to food or keeping herself busy, as she recalled, "I actually made myself sit on the couch and feel. It was so uncomfortable. I was in complete anxiety. I would cry a lot. All I wanted to do was go to the store and get ice cream." Instead, she literally sat on her hands, crying for hours. "I knew the only way to *get through* it was to *go through* it."

As Tracey continued to surrender, her understanding deepened. "I saw how my life's been controlled by fear. I've always had to feel like I was completely in control. What did I really have control over? But in my mind, control was safety."

Tracey discovered that buried under the intensity of raw emotion lies a cornucopia of wisdom, freedom, and ultimately, healing. On the other side of fear is where your power (and pleasure) lies.

"I now see control is such a false sense of security. I feel like I'm beginning to step into my power by being authentic," she said. "I had to break through all my unhealthy beliefs, labels, rules, regulations, busyness. I had to stop hiding and dig deep and feel the emotions, the pain, the anger, the shame and guilt, in order to get to this place I'm in now. I'm feeling so much better for excavating all of my skeletons from the closet. It has been quite the journey and one that I am proud I finally surrendered to in order to be where I am."

One woman realized after a *Sacred Success* retreat, "Surrendering is much harder than busyness, but a million times more powerful!"

Surrender Isn't Sedentary

"I rest in quiet certainty that I will do what is given me to do."

—A Course in Miracles

I spent much of my Surrender time in pj's, gazing out the window. But I also cleaned my closets, organized my files, downloaded tunes to my iPod, worked out at the gym, had regular massages, and joined a mastermind group. My boyfriend, Lee, moved in and we got engaged. We visited my oldest daughter in California and made plans to go to Sedona with friends. Not as a means of avoidance but as a way to nourish myself and have some fun.

A note of caution is in order: Watch out for escapist activity camouflaged as self-care. "I totally know the difference now," Erin wrote in an email, "between doing things from a place of busyness, just to avoid the discomfort of not knowing what comes next, versus doing it because oh yes, that totally adds to the joy of my life."

Surrender need not always be serious. I believe fun and joy factor heavily in healing. Mindy Goldstein bought crafts, like glitter, glue, and Magic Markers. "I'm not an artist, but I get great joy out of playing with arts and crafts," she said. "I want to be pleasure-seeking, not pain-avoiding. I've spent my life in pain avoidance. Now, I want to do things for the pure pleasure, for the joy, for the fun."

Tracey started going dancing with friends. "When I dance, I feel joy and I feel free," she told me, describing one particular evening. "I was having so much fun, just enjoying the music and my body, dancing like no one was in the room. Then all of a sudden I heard this little voice go, *'Welcome home, Tracey.'* I realized that's what I felt like as a four-year-old before all the abuse started happening."

Today Tracey says, "Stillness has been my gold mine. I found so many gems within that space. I can now see all the gifts. I feel like a different person, one who is authentic without all the masks."

When you stop incessant activity, you can discover your authentic self. As you eliminate the unnecessary, you learn what really matters. Once you put empty space in your day, various insights will begin to emerge. Slowing down actually speeds up the creative process.

"I'm convinced," I wrote in my journal, "as I continue to surrender, opportunities and ideas will arise. In fact, I'm counting on it. My job is just to do what's next, grabbing whatever the Universe tosses my way. I'm still in the thick of Surrender, but I swear, I see light at the end of the tunnel. I'm not sure what I'll find in that light. But I trust it will be glorious!"

About eight months into my sabbatical, I was looking out the window watching a pair of eagles soar, when I felt an unexpected surge of energy, a twinge of anticipation, as if something exciting was just around the corner. An idea emerged. "Maybe I'll do an intensive for women, a *Sacred Success* retreat," I wrote in my journal. "Maybe I'll even create a workbook for it."

Strangely, I didn't feel compelled to act immediately on this flash of clarity. I was trying a new tack, giving up exertion, replacing it with trust.

"She wasn't where she had been. She wasn't where she was going. But she was on her way." This quote from designer Jodi Hills, which popped up on Facebook soon afterward, aptly expressed how I felt at that moment.

Navigating Stage 2 in Four Simple Steps

"If you cannot hear the Voice for God, it is because you do not choose to listen."

—*A Course in Miracles*

Surrender is not passive, by any means. It is a state of inner activity, self-reflection being the major focus. I remember interviewing Marsha Firestone, president and founder of the Women Presidents' Organization, who told me emphatically: "You can't make adjustments in your behavior if you aren't first aware of what that behavior is. WPO isn't about making your business better. It's about making you better for your business."

The self-reflection you do in Stage 2 enables you to live a better, more purposeful and powerful life. As in the first stage, this one follows four steps. Be warned. You'll instinctively want to flip into busyness. That's how the Ego works. Just do your best to stay receptive to your Soul's quiet counsel. Again, begin by asking yourself a question.

STEP 1: ASK YOURSELF: WHO AM I?

"It's taken me a really long time to embrace my ambition and accept it in a loving way as part of who I am instead of putting myself down for it."

—*Kyra Sedgwick*

The whole point of asking "Who am I?" is to get in touch with all parts of yourself—your light, your darkness, the misconceptions you've had about yourself, all those self-imposed blocks you didn't even know were self-imposed. This question's sole function is to help you learn to love and accept all those parts you once judged harshly, kept hidden, put down, or deemed false.

Determining the answer to this question, however, can be daunting. Many of us have spent a lifetime hiding our real self from others. Consequently, we've lost touch with who we really are. We're left with self-fabricated illusions, behind which lie an array of unconscious decisions we've made about ourselves and life—usually when we were very young—that have nothing to do with reality. Yet we go through life acting on these arbitrary conclusions as if they were indisputable truths.

"I am peeling off the layers, tearing down the walls, digging really, really deep in search of ME as ME, not as the creation of a dysfunctional family," Molly, an attorney in the throes of divorce, told me after the retreat. "I am good at taking care of others but only now am I learning to take care of myself, to identify my needs and desires and then act on that information. I am learning that it is not selfish to do what I want to do when I want to do it. I am identifying behavior that no longer serves, and eliminating it from my repertoire."

That's precisely the work we need to do in Stage 2—identify all those early decisions and erroneous beliefs that give rise to dysfunctional behavior and a dissatisfying life, and that no longer serve us. We also need to identify, being brutally honest, all our skills, strengths, talents, and gifts, those marvelous attributes we frequently dismiss or devalue.

I asked myself this question—who am I *really*?—over and over again while journaling, meditating, staring out the window, sometimes processing my insights with friends. I even asked people who knew me: What do you see in me that I don't see in myself? I invite you to do the same.

STEP 2: CLARIFY YOUR PURPOSE.

"Let yourself be silently drawn by the stronger pull of what you really love."

—Rumi

Remember, *Sacred Success* is purpose driven, not profit driven. Every successful high earner I interviewed possessed an almost divine sense of mission, a transpersonal commitment to something larger than herself. This is what sets the Great apart from the mainstream.

As Napoleon Hill declared in his classic study of wealthy individuals, *Think and Grow Rich*, "There is one quality which one must possess to win, and that is definiteness of purpose, the knowledge of what one wants and a burning desire to possess it."

There's a significant difference between drive and addiction, however. Drive comes from a vision that nourishes our Soul and enriches our life. Addiction arises from the Ego's fear-based beliefs, such as scarcity, inadequacy, and shame, and it inevitably leads to burnout.

A flourishing venture capitalist told me, "I had a massive inner critic and I pushed myself until I broke down. By doing lots of self-improvement work, I figured out how to achieve my dream without killing myself."

Our purpose can only be found outside our comfort zone, beyond the Ego's fiefdom of all that's familiar. Busyness, therefore, is the Ego's attempt to avoid this step. The Ego knows a strong sense of purpose generates an inexorable persistence in a way that money alone never can.

One mega-earner put it this way: "Having a big vision creates the drive to do something meaningful in a big way."

And another agreed: "I have such a deep sense of mission and purpose that I go into full throttle, even in volunteer work."

Whenever these women were scared, stymied, or facing a seemingly insurmountable obstacle, as they often were, they consciously harkened back to their higher purpose. "When in doubt," a multimillion-dollar earner said to me, "I revisit my mission: Why am I here?"

Your purpose is your true north, especially important when you're navigating turbulent seas. To help me remember this, I keep a quote from Joan of Arc near my desk: "I am not afraid. I was born to do this." That's how a higher purpose feels. You *must* do this, no matter what happens, no matter how frightened you are, no matter how impossible it seems. This is what you were born to do. In the context of a purpose, "I want to" becomes "I HAVE to."

You may or may not know your purpose. My suggestion: Come with an empty cup and a willingness to think BIG. For generations, women have been groomed to play small, but that's not how *Sacred Success* is played. Compromising yourself by lowering your sights, going for what seems "reasonable," is the antithesis of Greatness.

I'd long assumed my purpose was to empower women financially. That's been my passion for decades. But I took the advice of Joseph Campbell: "We must be willing to let go of the life we have planned so as to have the life that is waiting for us." I was more than willing. I was eager.

During Receptive Surrender, I let go of my business in general and my identity in particular to discover who I really was and why I was here. After a lifetime of struggling to be something I felt I wasn't, I was ready for a considerably different approach.

Purposes can range from the unquestionably ambitious (create world peace) to the seemingly trivial (lead a simple life).

Erin, who was originally aghast at the idea of doing nothing, stubbornly resisted Surrender until she finally caved in and spent two days alone at her grandmother's cabin. "I walked the mountains. I wrote a lot. I went through the journals I've kept over the last eight years. I saw there was clearly a pattern, how much I loved teaching and helping young women. And I just haven't done anything about it," she confessed. "I realized I needed to chart a new path."

Erin's purpose, she realized, is to support women in living their truth. Mindy's is to spread magic, joy, and fun. Melanie's is to awaken the healer within oneself. Mine, inspired by a Mother Teresa quote, is to be a pencil in God's hand. Empowering women financially is how I accomplish my purpose. But, as I realized during my time in Surrender, my true purpose is spiritual, to act from a desire to serve, not from an unquenchable need to feel important.

When Suzy Carroll, who owns a nutrition store, came to the *Sacred Success* retreat, she said, "I felt like a piece of Suzy was missing. I went searching for this elusive piece of me, by looking deep into my Soul for what makes me buzz, what bothers me, what revs me up, and what brings me peace." But after completing a series of exercises (I've included them at the end of this chapter), she said, "it became as clear as day that my purpose is to motivate and inspire. I didn't need to be an expert, as I felt I should. Just writing the words 'inspire' and 'motivate' brings on that 'buzzing' feeling in me."

As a result, she said, "I happily put away all the materials I had been studying on my quest to become a Holistic Health Practitioner (memorizing herbs—total blah for me) and jumped (more like dive-bombed) with all my heart and Soul into teaching. I'm a much happier person now, calmer, more balanced."

That's when she noticed: "People began appearing in my life who offered wisdom, guidance, and helped direct me along a path to a deeper connection and understanding of 'me.'"

This is precisely what happens when we clarify our purpose—angels appear, the way is shown, and opportunities occur, often disguised as coincidences. Our job is to recognize and receive these gifts fully.

STEP 3: RECEIVE EVERYTHING, CONSCIOUSLY AND UNCONDITIONALLY.

> *"Make no attempt to judge anything because you do not understand what anything means . . . all meaning comes from your past experience."*
>
> —*A Course in Miracles*

Receiving is something most of us, women in particular, are not very good at. Yet I've come to see there's a direct correlation between our level of success and our ability to receive.

The *Course* tells us, "*Every day a thousand treasures come to me with every passing moment.*" Our job is to open our eyes, as well as our hearts, to fully receive those copious treasures. Too often we let the distractions of daily life, as well as our yammering Egos, prevent us from noticing what's being laid at our feet. Ignoring the bounty that flows to us is, essentially, an act of pushing it away, of saying "no" to abundance (in whatever form it may take). Why would we ever do that?

Because, as Charlene, the VP of finance, explained to me in an email, "Receiving love, receiving affluence, and receiving all the things I truly want is scary. I risk being vulnerable and getting hurt. But not receiving these things means living an unsatisfying life. And so the only real choice for me is to face the fear of being hurt in my vulnerability so that I can grow in love and affluence, which will result in greater happiness."

Receiving is to our Soul what eating is to our bodies—a source of strength, nourishment, and growth. To gain the benefits from food, we must chew, swallow, digest. So too, there are three steps to receiving: acknowledge, appreciate, and assimilate. When you don't fully engage in each of the three steps, you starve your Soul.

For myself, I began observing how often I glossed over words of praise or gratitude, without really absorbing or appreciating them fully. So I started what I called a Receiving Journal, separate from my daily journal. This was so powerful that I commissioned Tara Dixon, a magnificent artist and *Sacred Success* graduate, to design a Receiving Journal that I give to everyone who attends my retreat.

Keeping a Receiving Journal heightens your awareness. It forces you to acknowledge, appreciate, and assimilate the gifts being offered to you every day.

"The act of writing things down," a woman commented in an email after the retreat, "helps me receive, experience, and appreciate wonderful things that otherwise would just blip off my consciousness like a pebble on the surface of a lake."

Create your own Receiving Journal where you keep notes of all the treasures that come your way: an acknowledgment on Twitter, a kiss on the cheek, a significant insight, or an accurate hunch.

Here's where it gets tricky. Many gifts come disguised and are easily overlooked. To receive *consciously* and *unconditionally*, you must *suspend judgment*. That means you must reframe your challenges. Nothing that happens is "good" or "bad," "right" or "wrong," "negative" or "positive." It is far more valuable to see everything, absolutely everything, as useful information—a sign, a message, a lesson, or a form of Divine communication.

"*In order to judge anything rightly,*" says the *Course*, "*one would have to be fully aware of an inconceivably wide range of things: past, present and to come.*" Judgment, the *Course* explains, "*always rests on the past.*"

Even if we can't know what everything means at the moment, conscious receiving requires you to see all problems, obstacles, or challenges (regardless of how they feel) not in light of your past problems, but as support for your future desires. Success and failure are simply feedback systems, supporting you in staying on track.

This is counterintuitive, for sure. It's easy to receive a compliment from a friend, but a reprimand from your boss? This too can be a gift when you mine it for its deeper meaning.

"Problems don't exist for me," said one very successful woman, who tried to set up a meeting with Hillary Clinton but was repeatedly rebuffed. "It's all an opportunity to make it work. In fact, when somebody says 'I can't,' I think, 'Okay, here's an opportunity.'" She was not at all surprised when she eventually got the meeting.

"My successes have come from my challenges," said another woman, whose company went bankrupt when her business partner was sent to prison for embezzlement. Nonetheless, she refused to use the word "problem" or even "obstacle." "'Growth opportunities' is a better word," she told me.

The challenge is to find the treasure in what may seem terrible, to look for the gift in every situation, even if it feels "bad." I continue to hone this skill in myself, looking at how everything I judge "distasteful" could actually be a springboard to my desires—in all aspects of my life. It's not easy, and when I feel stuck, I turn a line from the *Course* into a prayer: *"Above all else, I want to see this differently."* Remember, shifting your perception is the secret to creating miracles.

For example, I had a big fight with my boyfriend. Rather than stewing in my anger (okay, I did that for a while), I actually stopped, repeated my prayer and then asked myself: *How can I use this to take me higher?* (This phrase helps me start reframing.) As I searched for what this spat had to teach me, I discovered I was repeating a pattern that had messed up all my other relationships. That insight went into my Receiving Journal. And I'm so grateful I caught it. Lee and I are now happily married.

In *Sacred Success*, to quote a Zen saying, "the obstacle is the path." Every problem is, in truth, a source of guidance, support, and strength building. A good example is a conversation I had with insurance executive Erin the day after her phone system shut down in the middle of a very busy period.

Instead of lamenting her circumstances, she said, "I saw it as a huge 'Stop Doing' sign. My body was really tired and wanted to relax. Rather than jumping in to fix the problem, I let my team handle it. I went for a long walk, scheduled a ninety-minute massage, and took a midafternoon nap. Today I'm refreshed and ready 'to do.' I feel super productive and I'm getting more done in less time! That's what I call a gift!"

The fact is, from our current vantage point we really don't know what anything means or how it will affect us in the future. The *Course* expresses it beautifully: "*What would you not accept if you knew that everything that happens, all events, past, present and to come are gently planned by One whose only purpose is your good?*"

Take Carmel Dean, musical director of a Broadway show. When her show was canceled after only three weeks, she went into shock. "You always think your show is going to be the next big thing—or at least stay open for a decent amount of time! I have been through such myriad emotions," she wrote me in an update. But the morning after she received the closing notice, she continued, "I got a random email from someone I haven't seen in ten years, who told me she was now teaching musical theatre in Paris, and if I was ever over that way to tell her so I could teach a master class there. HELLO!!! I was going to Paris in two weeks, and because I don't have to get back to the show anymore, I've been able to extend my trip and will now be hosting a master class and possibly even a cabaret of my own music. In PARIS!!"

STEP 4: OBEY THE LAW OF OWNERSHIP.

"That which you wish to hide or change is your power."

—*Fame*

In *Sacred Success*, we take conscious receiving one step further. We must claim what we receive as rightfully ours by obeying the Law of Ownership, which says: *Unless you officially own something, it's not yours to keep. Ownership signifies permanent status. Otherwise, you're borrowing, leasing, renting, or caretaking—which implies possession can be taken away.*

Greatness requires that we own our worth, our power, our talent, and our truths. This was clear in my interviews with high earners. As one told me, "My millions are a reflection of my value, my mirror."

Too many of us devalue ourselves and dismiss our accomplishments, and every time we don't own our successes—by slipping into self-depreciation, denying a compliment, or refusing to believe we deserve more—we are giving our power away.

If you don't own what you already have, how will you ever create more? Moreover, if you don't value what you own, you'll likely lose it. Greatness is drawn to us by obeying the Law of Ownership, owning and appreciating everything we bring to the table. The more you can appreciate what you have or the progress you've made, even if it's only a teeny-tiny bit, the more Greatness you'll likely attract. I always try to praise myself for any progress I've made, no matter how minuscule. "Good job, Barbara," I'll say, when I do something I dread, even if it doesn't go well. I'm proud of myself for at least doing it!

Often, we don't just deny our potential, but also project it onto another person or thing, real or imagined, and see them as having what we lack. *"Denial of power always results in projection,"* the *Course* tells us. *"What you project, you disown and do not believe is yours."*

It's not uncommon to deny traits we don't like about ourselves by projecting them onto others so we can make *them* wrong. However, we also project our assets and our power onto others, absolving ourselves of any responsibility to use them. As I wrote in an earlier book, "Prince Charming is but our own potential waiting to be developed." Understanding our projections, says author Gary Zukav, "is the first step of authentic power."

Ownership means owning our mistakes and misperceptions, our false beliefs and bad behaviors, along with our talents, skills, and accomplishments—not to beat ourselves up, but to hold ourselves accountable. Everything in our past has made us who we are today.

As Luci, who plays keyboard in a rock band, finally realized: "I must also trust my mistakes, my nervousness, my shakiness, and my accidents. Because so often it's through accidents that I create my favorite part of a song, sing the most emotive line, or channel the me-est me."

EXERCISE: The Reclamation Project

In the first column, make a list of people you admire, envy, love, respect, or wish you were like. In the second column, list their qualities. Now take a look at that list and realize that you own everything on that list. Can you accept these qualities as yours?

Names	Qualities

When I got this email from Tracey Allred, the former TV producer, I knew she too was well on her way to healing: "I'm allowing whatever needs to come up and I'm owning it all," she wrote. "I no longer want to hide. I'm ready to own my shit to find my true power. The anger and rage. The good girl and the bad girl. My many masks. My pseudo protection. My accomplishments. My words. My actions. Everything that has to do with me. I am grateful for all this awareness. I own it all. And I LOVE every morsel of myself."

Moving On

"In quietness are all things answered and is every problem solved."

—A Course in Miracles

As the ninth month of my sabbatical rolled around, I wrote in my journal: "I suspect my time spent in Surrender is drawing to a close. I'm walking away with a whole new appreciation for downtime and empty space. But just recently, I've been sensing a shift. My energy seems to be changing."

I realized that the nine months spent in Surrender had turned into a period of gestation. Despite feeling as if nothing was happening, I had actually been quite busy creating a new body of work. Like a proud mama, it was now time for me to take my "baby" out into the world.

Near the end of that nine-month sabbatical, in early August 2010— six weeks before my first *Sacred Success* retreat—I woke up at 5 A.M. due to a noisy sprinkler system. Immediately, I began receiving Downloads from the Divine. My man turned over to see me staring at the ceiling, eyes opened.

"Shhh," I said, "I'm downloading."

This went on for four consecutive mornings. I spent the afternoons typing up the information I received. Every new piece of data added a deeper layer to what I got the day before. I knew it was time to integrate these layers into a curriculum. Two days later, I had a final draft of a workbook.

On September 23, I gave my first four-day *Sacred Success* retreat. I called it my coming-out party. The event was extraordinary. I felt more alive and motivated than I had in years. I was bursting with new ideas, excited to bring each one to fruition.

I was squarely in Stage 3 of *Sacred Success*: Disciplined Action.

CHAPTER SUMMARY: Receptive Surrender—Stage 2

- Rather than ignoring the Call and risking a crisis, choose Receptive Surrender by taking time to reflect and regroup.

- Surrender is a highly underrated practical strategy to ensure you're proceeding in the direction of Greatness rather than spinning your wheels chasing mediocrity.

- The Soul requires stillness so you can hear the secrets it yearns to share.

- Stillness and empty space give rise to painful feelings. Rather than experience the pain, busyness becomes your drug of choice.

- The whole point of Receptive Surrender is to finally release what you've been repressing. To heal you must feel.

- Surrender is challenging for everyone, but for those who've suffered abuse, the experience is exceptionally grueling, the Ego intensely resistant.

- When you face your demons, you begin to notice a connection between your emotions and your power. Suppressing one inhibits expressing the other.

- Slowing down actually speeds up the creative process.

- You navigate Stage 2 in four steps:
  - Step 1: Ask yourself: Who am I?
  - Step 2: Clarify your purpose.
  - Step 3: Receive everything, consciously and unconditionally.
  - Step 4: Obey the Law of Ownership.

STAGE 2 HOMEWORK

Here are four exercises to help you find your purpose.

EXERCISE: Where to Look for Your Purpose

Here are four places to help you find—or redefine—your purpose:

1. In Past Pain

In an early draft of my first book, *Prince Charming Isn't Coming*, my editor cut this line because she considered it corny: "In our deepest pain lies our highest purpose." I'm not sure our life purpose has to come from pain, but it's a good place to start looking. *What has been your most painful challenge in life?*

2. In World Problems

Back in graduate school, someone asked me, "If you had a magic wand, what one thing would you change on this planet?" I knew immediately: I'd liberate women to work as equals among men. It was the seventies! Very soon after, I got a job at the women's center on campus, helping women reentering the workforce. That put me on the path to where I am today. Look around . . . *What global problem do you feel strongly about? How can you contribute to the solution?* What is the one problem in the world that you'd be willing to spend the next ten years of your life working on, talking about, and being part of the solution to? Is there a world problem for which finding a solution is a "*have* to" for you, not a "*want* to"?

---

3. In Childhood Play

When I was little, I played school with my sisters. Of course I was the teacher. Later I organized a neighborhood camp, and I was the sole counselor. As I grew older, I dreamed of becoming a college professor. I had babies instead. As we look back at the tapestry of our lives, it's easy to spot certain threads that continually repeat, displaying an unwavering pattern holding clues to our purpose. *What did you love to play as a kid?*

4. In Secret Wishes

Think about those pipe dreams you've never told anyone about because they're so absurd, it's embarrassing. Mine was to be a rock star. (Oh God, it's true!) Once, someone asked me: "If you could do anyone's job, whose would it be?" That was easy. Neil Diamond's. Why? The words just slipped out: "I want to write my songs and sing them." This phrase resonated so deeply, I've let it guide me through a myriad of careers. Okay, so I can't carry a tune. But I've managed to write my songs (books) and sing (teach) them. *If you could have anyone's job, whose would it be?*

EXERCISE: Meditation with the Wise One

Close your eyes, take several deep breaths, and relax your whole body. Feel the relaxation flow through every part of you—from your head, down your neck and shoulders, your torso, buttocks, and legs, your feet, and toes. You are now fully relaxed.

Imagine that you are sitting in a safe place. It could be real or imagined, indoors or outside. As you sit there, you see your Wise One approaching. Welcome your Wise One, the keeper of all knowledge and the Divine purpose for your life.

Ask the Wise One: "Who am I? Why am I here?" And listen for what the Wise One has to tell you. Ask again until you get a response.

You may or may not understand what you're told, though you may ask for clarification. Just trust that what you get is exactly what you need to hear.

Then the Wise One hands you a gift. Accept it. Again, if you're not clear what it means, ask for clarification. If none comes, rest assured you'll eventually understand the meaning. When you're ready, write down what the Wise One told you.

EXERCISE: The Three Big Questions

Below are three powerful questions. Read the first one. Then close your eyes and pay attention to whatever comes to mind. Do not dismiss or force anything! Write down your response. Then move on to the second question, until you've completed all three. Were there any surprises or new discoveries?

1. **If I found out I had six months to live, where would I go? Who would I be with? What would I be doing?**

2. **If I died today, what would be left unlived?**

3. **If nothing at all changed, what will my life look like in five years?**

EXERCISE: My Purpose Statement

Write a first draft of your purpose statement. You may start with: "My purpose is to . . ." It doesn't have to be worded perfectly. What matters is its visceral effect on you. Whatever you write can be changed or modified later. Nothing is set in stone.

Use these questions for guidance: *What do I dearly want to accomplish? What was I born to do? Who do I want to help? What are my talents? How do I want to live? What is the outcome I want to create?*

This is only a first draft. You will be revising it many times, so don't worry about saying it exactly the right way.

CHAPTER 5

Disciplined Action—Stage 3

"There is nothing that you cannot do."

—*A Course in Miracles*

The D Word

"In the last analysis, our only freedom is the freedom to discipline ourselves."

—*Bernard Baruch*

I was finally in the action stage, eager to shift into high gear. Soon after my first *Sacred Success* retreat, I hired a team and we hit the ground running. We restructured my website, developed a marketing campaign, purchased complicated software, attracted new clients, created all sorts of new products. After a few months, however, my enthusiasm began to wane and I found myself bordering on burnout yet again.

This took me by surprise. I thought for sure I was done with Surrender, ready to move on. Why was I being called to slow down once more—and so soon? The answer came, loud and clear, when I visited my youngest daughter, an organic farmer. One of her chores was pruning the fruit trees.

"If you don't prune back most of the new buds," Anna explained, "too much of the tree's energy goes into producing foliage instead of growing fruit. You don't want the trees to spread themselves too thin, reducing the amount of fruit they bear."

The metaphor was inescapable. I was that fruit tree, spreading myself too thin, letting too many budding projects sap my creativity, my energy, my focus. A part of me was scared to cut back. The other part knew I had to.

I imagined my Soul smiling patiently as I worked myself into a frenzy. On my return from the farm, I received the "gift" of pneumonia, an indisputable signal I needed to Surrender. But this time, my respite was only for a brief duration, long enough to learn a noteworthy lesson.

While Disciplined Action and Receptive Surrender may be separate stages, they operate in tandem, like dance partners. Sitting in stillness entails discipline. Likewise, Disciplined Action—consistent activity in the direction of your desire—requires time for reflection. No wonder I burned out. I hadn't stopped long enough to notice I had way too many balls in the air. I let my bliss get swallowed up by busyness.

This is an occupational hazard for high achievers. I constantly warn women that Disciplined Action means *doing with discernment*, thoughtfully pruning rather than tirelessly pushing.

"Although I've been deluged with work over the last three weeks," Suzanne Hanger said about her real estate career, "I was able to balance it with journaling, yoga, and meditation. I paid attention to when I'd had enough and took off on a hike. This felt odd, as I typically keep working until all the work is done."

Though it may have felt odd, she was delighted with the outcome. "I am clearer about my next steps, energized by the work, and optimistic that great things are to come," she reported happily.

In our culture, however, the notion of discipline is about as unpopular—and as misunderstood—as the idea of Surrender. Both are often regarded with disdain. While Surrender is seen as squandering time, discipline is often viewed as a loss of freedom, a form of punishment, an unpleasant obligation, or an impossible virtue. Even after attending three retreats, Canadian executive Charlene White refuses to even utter the word, she dislikes it that much.

I sometimes wonder if we instinctively recoil from discipline, like a kid ordered to eat veggies. It may be good for us, but damn it, we're not going to like it and we'll try anything to get out of it.

"I used to pray for discipline. I thought if I prayed hard enough and long enough, one day I'd have it," Oprah once said about losing weight. "But it wasn't until I made the decision to be true to my word that my prayers were answered. I began to work out every morning whether I liked it or not. And before long I started to behave and look like a disciplined person."

Discipline comes from the Latin word *discipul*, meaning "*being a disciple unto oneself*." The work at this stage is to become your own biggest fan, viewing yourself in the very best light, being kind to yourself when things don't go well, doing what you may not be keen to do, but doing it anyway because the payoff is so rewarding. In *Sacred Success*, discipline is a source of pleasure, the essence of power, and the path to Greatness. One woman labeled it "'*Blissipline*' since the results make you so happy."

"I have moved through the Call to Greatness to Receptive Surrender and am now emerging into Disciplined Action," announced professional musician Luci. "I am ready to be my biggest fan by taking daily action. I've developed a Disciplined Action Plan: Write four hours a day, no matter where I am and what is happening around me." During her "Music Boot Camp," Luci wrote forty songs in ten days.

"It wasn't all fun," she admitted. "I got upset on day three because I hated doing the work. Which triggered an old story for me: 'Oh no, if I hate it it's because I can't do it. What if I'm not good enough?' But then I realized this is what will set me apart from every other musician. It takes time and focused daily work to become Great. When I realized this, the heaviness lifted off my chest and writing has been much easier."

The Mind-Set for Stage 3

"Self discipline begins with the mastery of your thoughts. If you don't control what you think, you can't control what you do."

—*Napoleon Hill*

Disciplined Action stems from Disciplined Thinking. Without question, our mind-set, the way we think, determines our behavior, the choices we make, and the results we create. Mental discipline is the key to sustaining Disciplined Action.

"What you do comes from what you think," the *Course* tells us. *"You must change your mind, not your behavior."* Otherwise, warns the *Bhagavad Gita*, "The mind acts like an enemy for those who don't control it."

I once read a University of Pennsylvania study finding that the average person thinks 50,000 thoughts a day, 70 percent of which are negative. In my interviews with women making millions, I witnessed how vigilantly they practiced mental discipline by resisting negative dialogue.

One of them explained it to me like this: "You have to be disciplined about the way you think, which means paying attention to every word that goes in your mind and out your mouth." She compared this task of mental monitoring to the time she quit biting her nails. "When I caught myself doing it, I just stopped."

These women carefully observed their conversations (internal and external), making sure they didn't lapse into negative patterns of thought or speech—or stopping themselves when they did. This is particularly challenging for women, who tend to instinctively diminish themselves at every turn.

High earners are no different. Almost all those I interviewed confessed to feeling insecure and incompetent. Yet, they forced themselves (until it became a habit) to consciously censor negative chatter by focusing on their strengths and successes, talking about their achievements to others, reaffirming their value to themselves, and recasting problems as opportunities.

I call this technique "Constructive Denial," which means focusing entirely on your strengths, your value, everything you bring to the table, while denying the Ego's lies about how small, inadequate, or inconsequential you are.

"I have to constantly remind myself, I'm okay. I have strengths," one mega-earner admitted. "It's hard. But I know what keeps women back is a mind-set of inadequacy."

"I don't use the word 'can't,'" another told me. "And I started fining my people a dollar every time they did."

Language is powerful. There is a direct correlation between what you think, the words you use, and the life you have. If you want to change your life, change your story.

Mental discipline rests heavily on the self-awareness you gained in the previous stage. You can't change anything if you don't know it exists.

Years ago, my business coach, Margery Miller, gave me an assignment to observe my conversations with others. I saw how I habitually put myself down. I'd dismiss my skills ("Oh, that's no big thing"), deflect praise ("I thought I was awful"), and diminish my successes ("But I could've done so much better").

"Self-depreciation is your comfort zone," Margery told me. She was right. What felt, to me, like humility, was actually reinforcing my insecurity and eroding my confidence. A surprising number of successful women told me they had similar experiences.

"I had to quit saying 'I'm not a businesswoman,'" a former journalist recalled. "That's how I held myself back. I knew I had to stop putting myself down, so I started saying, 'I'm a *great* businesswoman.'"

"*Denial is as capable of being used positively as well as negatively,*" insists *A Course in Miracles*. "*Forgetting what you are not enables you to remember what you are.*"

"I have spent years and years and years telling myself I am not good enough. It is such a comfortable and familiar story that I hardly realized

I was doing it," Luci told me. "Self-bashing is comfortable, but definitely not fun. I now live in this story: 'I am good enough. In fact, I am amazing.' Living in this story is way more fun."

Constructive Denial is *not* about denying negative emotions, but disciplining yourself to feel them so you can release them. For example, when strategic planner and meeting facilitator Tatiana Bredikin endured a major setback at work, she told me, "I felt how this 'failure' is tied to all my past failures. After a mere fifteen minutes of consciously choosing to experience the full weight of these feelings, they were released. I was then peaceful and immediately knew the solution."

Can you see that mental discipline (all discipline, in fact) is, in effect, an act of self-love? Tracey, the former TV producer, let her bills pile up when she lost her job. She was finally ready to face them after her retreat. "There's a part of me that could go and beat myself up about it," she said. "But I've beat myself up enough over the last forty years; I don't need to do it any longer. So what I'm telling myself now is 'you're doing the best you can, and you're learning.' I'm really proud of myself for that."

That's exactly what mental discipline sounds like—taking pride in your tiniest successes, as well as giving yourself pep talks, repeating positive affirmations, surrounding yourself with supportive people, pinning up inspirational sayings.

When Natalia Volz, a single mother of three, saw a quote by author Lynn Grabhorn, "Problems give meaning to a life without purpose," she embraced it as a personal edict. "I started making an effort to talk more about my purpose," Natalia said. "It's much more fun and exhilarating. Ideas flow from talking about our purpose. Connections grow out of talking about it. Next steps open up. When I get on purpose, I get off of problems."

Are you doing something similar—minimizing your achievements, underestimating your value, or focusing on the negative? I invite you, for the next few days, to simply pay attention, observing your thoughts and conversations. Don't change anything, just notice. Then ask yourself this question: *Could I be holding myself back by what I'm telling myself or sharing with others?* What you share with another, you strengthen in yourself.

Every time I heard me belittling myself, I stopped. Literally stopped, midsentence, and forced myself to say something positive, even if it was merely "thank you." At first, it felt weird and awkward. But gradually, as I kept practicing positivity, I began to notice that what started as a conscious practice eventually became an unconscious habit.

When I talked to Melanie, the energy healer, just before her seminar, I asked how she was feeling about leading a large group for the very first time. She responded as the embodiment of mental discipline.

"I've learned I can flip the coin from anxiety to excitement," she exclaimed. "This is a first for me. I can be really scared or really excited! I choose to plug into my excited Soul versus my fearful Ego."

EXERCISE: Create a *Sacred Success* Affirmation

Affirmations can be a very powerful form of mental discipline. An affirmation is a short statement, declaring what you want as if it's already yours. Write them down. Post them in full view. Say them out loud as often as possible. You can program your brain by silently repeating the statement throughout the day.

For example, some affirmations I often use are: "I see only my value." "Everything always works out for me." "I am powerful." "I am responsible with money."

To create your own affirmation, think about what you want to have or how you want to feel, and write your affirmations here. I have read that prefacing your intention with the words "I am" is particularly powerful because what follows that phrase can radically influence your reality.

Why Is Discipline Important?

*"You can never conquer the mountain. You can only
conquer yourself."*

—Jim Whittaker

Mental discipline is particularly crucial because success can be a
very emotional process for women. "It's not the business problems,"
explained Marsha Firestone. "It's the emotional turmoil that's the biggest challenge."

Success often defies self-image. Many women find themselves
thinking, "This isn't me," as their star begins to rise. Others struggle
with guilt, wondering, "Do I deserve this?" Practically every woman
wrestles with fear and self-doubt.

I was surprised how often successful women made the same gener-
alization: In the world of work, men feel entitled and are sure everyone
knows it, so they tend to take bigger risks. Women feel flawed, certain
everyone sees it, and so tend to hold back. Almost all those I interviewed
at some point felt like a fraud, afraid everyone would find out.

All it may take is one small mistake, one critical comment, to trigger
our insecurities and throw us off track. Without the mental discipline
to reassure and reassert ourselves, Ego will easily take over, exhorting
us to throw in the towel and hightail it to safety.

Natalia Volz ran a design firm founded by her husband, who died
three years before we met. Design was not her passion. But the firm was
her only source of income. After four days at the *Sacred Success* retreat,
she felt strongly called to become a grief coach and educator. When she
shared her dream with her father, he disapproved, pointing out that she
lacked credentials and would never make a living from it.

"I was flattened," she said, sighing heavily. "My father loves me, he
really does. But he brings me back to what I've heard my whole life. 'Be
careful, it's dangerous, I'm afraid for you. The world is not a kind place.'"

Rather than deferring to her Ego and admitting defeat, she exercised mental discipline by telling herself that these were her father's fears, not fact or reality.

"As [my father] spoke, a tiny spark within reminded me that I am to follow *my* heart's desire now. If I am to live my joy, then I must continue," she said, adding, "I need to be careful who I share my enthusiasm with at this time."

Natalia dove headfirst into Disciplined Action. She took a training program in grief work, announced to her kids' school that she was a grief recovery specialist interested in starting a parent group, and volunteered at a hospice, which quickly assigned her a client.

"Oh my God! I felt so excited and nervous," she recalled after meeting the client. "My Soul was dancing such a joyful dance. My Ego yelled and screamed that I am not qualified, ready, able to coach someone through their grief. I did it anyway. The greatest feeling is doing work I am here to do right now. It is so right."

One of the keys to mental discipline is deliberately tuning into your Soul's passion while tuning out your Ego's fear. "I am scared," Natalia admitted at the time. "How will I make a living doing this? But I feel so drawn to this work. I have to keep myself in the present moment of excitement."

After a while, Natalia stumbled upon the exhilarating secret of Disciplined Action. "My fear was larger than the reality," she said, smiling. "Isn't that always the case? Action feels so much better than being paralyzed in fear. Fear shrinks through action."

Almost a year later, Natalia wrote to update me: "I got my first paying grieving client a month after discovering my calling at the retreat. I closed the design firm. The hospice where I've been volunteering offered me a part-time paying position as their bereavement coordinator (without me even asking. They approached me!). It's perfect because I am getting experience, exposure, money, and I still have time to work on my own business, which is where I can make some serious money and make the difference I really want to make. I feel such joy when I work and it comes so easily to me."

Four Steps to Disciplined Action

"The question isn't who's going to let me; it's who is going to stop me."

—*Ayn Rand*

As Natalia's story shows, fear fades with action. But not all actions are created equal. As I learned firsthand, we need to be wary of falling into scattered, frantic, or random activity. Busyness is basically the absence of discipline. In Disciplined Action, we make prudent, sometimes unpleasant choices, carefully selecting where to focus our attention. As with the prior stages, we take action by following four steps, beginning with the big question.

STEP 1: ASK YOURSELF: HOW WILL I PURSUE MY PURPOSE?

"Once the 'what' is decided, the 'how' always follows. We must not make 'how' an excuse for facing and accepting the 'what.'"

—*Pearl S. Buck*

Don't be fooled by the wording of this first question. It's not asking you to figure out every step or be fully prepared before you begin. Quite the contrary. Nearly every successful woman I've interviewed has told me her eventual success was more often due to providence than a premeditated plan.

A few years ago, I read an article about Condoleezza Rice and wrote down her words: "I never sat down and thought, 'I'll major in political science and Soviet studies, get a PhD, become a professor, serve in the first Bush administration, become provost at Stanford, and then become

National Security Advisor.' Not planning has permitted me to accept the twists and turns."

Similarly, a high earner in her forties explained: "One of the most important things I've learned is to just show up and be open to opportunities that come your way. At the time, you might not even know what they are."

"I just followed the unfolding," recalled a woman who has run a million-dollar business for over thirty years. "There were a lot of lucky breaks, and I followed them all."

This question—how will I pursue my purpose?—helps you carefully discern which of the "lucky breaks," chance meetings, and random opportunities align with your purpose, and which would lead you astray. I once saw a phrase in the *Wall Street Journal* that superglued itself to my brain: *the survival of the focused*. I have no recollection what the article was about, but I knew those five words told a powerful tale of surviving and thriving in our ever-changing world.

One woman in the retreat likened achieving success to mountain biking: "You can't be afraid when you are super focused in the moment."

I'm convinced that Greatness belongs to the focused. When life starts to get out of whack, as it often does, it usually means you've lost your focus. Without focus, it's easy to get sidetracked by irrelevant stuff that momentarily interests you, or the multiple fires fighting for your attention. But with focus, conflicting objectives cease to control you, making it easier (and less stressful) to take decisive action without second-guessing.

No matter how many opportunities or obligations await, Greatness demands you prioritize, then trim, your to-do list, because as the Roman philosopher Seneca said 2,000 years ago, "To be everywhere is to be nowhere."

I understand why people with lots of interests and skills often feel stymied. Focusing can be very frustrating for the multifaceted or multigifted. "The key is not to prioritize what's on your schedule," advised the late author Stephen R. Covey, "but to schedule your priorities."

Covey proffers a clear-cut formula for pursuing your purpose—focus exclusively on your priorities. Everything else is put on the back burner.

Every day, we are bombarded with a gazillion choices. Our current reality is the direct result of all the choices we've made up to this moment. If you want to change your reality, or some aspect of it, you need to be very clear about what you want and what you don't want and make sure your choices reflect the former.

As one high earner told me: "I think it's really important to take stock occasionally and remember why you're doing all of this. At the end of the day, what's really important? I am very clear on my priorities. So when balance sometimes gets out of whack, I focus on my personal priorities."

How do you even know what your priorities are? Most people haven't a clue. We carry around lengthy to-do lists, then feel stressed, guilty, or inadequate when we don't cross everything off—a surefire recipe for failure.

"I can have everything I want, just not all at one time," a *Sacred Success* graduate finally realized. "The key is to figure out what's most important." Here's a terrific exercise to help you do just that. I do this myself and often suggest it to clients.

EXERCISE: Prioritizing Everything on Your Plate

First, identify your top five values, what you cherish most in life. (Use the Values Clarification exercise, p. 130.)

Next, make a list of everything on your to-do list, all those items you simply *must* do. Write them in the space below and on the next page.

Finally, narrow your list down to five items, based on your most important values. These are your priorities. They take precedence when scheduling your time. *If it's not a priority, it's a distraction.*

1.

2.

3.

4.

5.

I'll never forget the panicked phone call I received from Athena Burke, a talented musician who belts out her original tunes at every *Sacred Success* retreat. "I'm in overwhelm," she said. I could hear the desperation in her voice. "I have a pattern of doing too much at once. I'm exhausted. And I've gained weight."

"Let's try this," I suggested. "Make a list of everything on your plate."

She came up with twenty-one items, including planning her wedding, moving into her fiancé's home, promoting her new CD, taking care of the kids during summer break, creating a website, not to mention cooking, shopping, watering the plants, and cleaning house. In Athena's world, all twenty-one items had equal weight! Nothing took precedence over anything else.

Next she wrote down her top five values. They were family, beautiful home, healing (resting and walking), singing, and building community.

Sifting everything through the filter of her most prized values, her priorities became obvious. She ranked them, in this order: walking, resting, kids, David, and singing. "I guess promoting my CD is off my plate, at least for the summer while the kids are out of school and I'm getting married," she said. She also realized she could delegate many of her chores to family members.

Suzy Carroll, the energetic but harried owner of a busy nutrition store, filled both sides of two pages with all the things she thought she should be doing. Then, she said, "I boiled down all my 'shoulds' to five priorities." We called it her "Detox Plan."

"This really helped me see what was important and what things I could let go," she said with relief. "You know, it wasn't complicated. It was simple things. Like when I get home from work take fifteen minutes for quiet time. My old habit was to come home, open all the mail, organize everything, pick up the kitchen. I was never stopping. Now I stop all the time.

"I think a lot of it had to do with what I deemed important in *my* mind. I had to do two newsletters every month, thinking my customers were really going to miss them if I didn't. Well, no, they wouldn't. My life would be so much better if I took them off my plate—so I did. In the past I never would have. And it's never backfired on me," she exclaimed about her Detox Plan. "Anything I chose to let go has never come back to bite me in the butt, ever!"

The trick to sticking to your priorities is maintaining clear boundaries. A boundary is essentially a strong YES or a strong NO.

"If it's not a 'HELL YES!'" explained Tracey, "Then I know it's a 'HELL NO!'"

But be aware that the YES is not to please people, as is the Ego's inclination. The YES is what lights *you* up, what your Soul craves, what you are meant to do. Your values and priorities determine when you say "yes," and when you say "no." If there are no boundaries, there's always anger.

When former TV producer turned stay-at-home-mom Cyndy Bragg got clear that her priorities were her family, time for herself, and her budding comedy career, she was able to say no to running for city council. Though the idea was appealing, local government wasn't a priority. "I had to ask myself, how am I going to feel if I'm overcommitted, and the answer was 'anxious and resentful.'"

Setting boundaries can be especially difficult for women. We're so used to putting everyone else's needs ahead of our own. But healthy boundaries are like oxygen masks on airplanes. We're in no shape to help anyone else until we take care of ourselves first.

"I have a compulsion to people-please," Stephanie Slawek, a yoga teacher, admitted. "I was raised with the belief that the worst thing I could *ever* do is upset someone—that would be worse than physically hurting them. Now that I am fully aware of this, I see it everywhere in my life. It almost feels like an actual force, like gravity, pulling me into pleaser-mode."

Slowly Stephanie began setting boundaries. "When I get an invitation, I stop and ask myself, do I really want to go, or do I want to make the host happy? When a client indicates that she doesn't like our appointment time, I stop and ask, do I want to try to rearrange? Would that make ME happy? When I sense that someone wants more from me than I want to give, instead of resenting it, I can stop and say to myself, 'they can want whatever they want. I am under no obligation to give it to them, unless it pleases me.' Oh, the liberation!"

Boundaries are both liberating and empowering. If you look at where you've given your power away (as we did in Stage 1), you'll likely see a lack of or very limp boundaries. If you don't establish strong boundaries, you can be sure other people will create them for you.

Molly, the attorney, who emailed me from Germany, finally realized, "I do not have to swoop in and play the heroine whenever someone needs me. Now I set boundaries so that I'm able to choose what is best for me under the circumstances, without guilt. I have said no to many requests or situations where previously I would have stepped in to express an opinion or otherwise get involved. I now understand that stuff happens, life is not always fair, we cannot control everything, and I do not have to save everyone I know or do not know. I preserve my own energy (and sense of well-being) when I choose my battles mindfully."

STEP 2: COMPLY WITH THE LAW OF GROWTH.

> *"I always did something I was a little not ready to do. I think that's how you grow. When there's that moment of 'Wow, I'm not really sure I can do this,' and you push through those moments, that's when you have a breakthrough."*
>
> —Marissa Mayer, CEO of Yahoo

The Law of Growth states that *everything in this Universe is either expanding or contracting, growing or shrinking. Otherwise it stagnates, dies, and/or disappears.* For all living things, growth occurs naturally. But we humans often unwittingly obstruct this organic process by heeding our Ego's urges to stay safe and play small. Resisting growth saddens our Soul but delights our Ego. In *Sacred Success*, our work is to continually stretch beyond the familiar by doing what we fear because that's the only way we'll ever reach Greatness.

In the words of Vincent van Gogh, "If you hear a voice within you say 'you cannot paint,' by all means paint and the voice will be silenced."

Every successful woman I've ever interviewed struggled with fear and self-doubt, but acted in spite of it. When I asked one woman the secret to her millions, she replied instantly "Not being concerned with having everything tucked and tied before jumping in. I may say I can't do something, but I always do."

Quite a few told me, as this one did, "I didn't know what the heck I was doing when I first started."

And "Oh yes, I was in fear," a serial entrepreneur said about her earliest business venture. "I just jumped in by the seat of my pants. I activated my deflector shield. I wasn't going to let anyone's bad energy get to me." When she didn't succeed, she recalled, "I picked myself up, dusted myself off, and said 'I will build a business. I will make a million. I will rebound.'" And rebound she did, starting a string of companies, many of which she sold for a fortune.

Marsha Firestone calls this the "fly-by-the-seat-of-your-pants school of management," which is very common among women in WPO because so many have had no business training. Some had no college degrees.

I call it "the stretch." As I discovered early on in my interviews with successful women, the number one requirement for achieving success in anything is the willingness to stretch beyond what feels comfortable to what seems impossible, to do what you don't want to do, what you think you can't do, or what just plain terrifies you. To grow you must stretch.

A few months after the retreat, Suzanne Hanger, the real estate agent we met earlier, decided to start an independent real estate brokerage and auction company. "I am excited and scared to death," she said. "The plan makes perfect sense and no sense at all. I am ready and not ready at the same time. If I'm successful, my income and opportunities will increase significantly. If I fail, I'll be in debt. It's a big leap. I think I'll take it." This is precisely how stretching feels.

While men tend to deny fear, too often women let fear control them. Growing and stretching is not about repressing fear, but reframing it, seeing it differently. The truth is, fear is nothing to fear. In fact, fear is good. Fear lets us know we're leaving our comfort zone on our way to Greatness. The only survival that's being threatened is our Ego's.

As advertising executive Victoria Edwards astutely declared during a retreat, "No one got anywhere being comfortable all the time!"

Nancy Black, a burned out doctor, came to the retreat hoping to revitalize her career. Instead, she went home and began dancing in shows. "A year ago when we started *Sacred Success*," she wrote in an update, "I would have said NO WAY would I ever perform. But when I performed on the cruise ship with my dance instructor, there are no words for how amazing it was. What I lacked in dance technique I made up for in pure joy! As soon as I hit the stage, my Soul turned to my Ego and said, 'I've got this one, step aside!!!' Forging ahead despite all my discomfort (and sometimes agony!) made me realize how great the joy is when you work through the discomfort!!! The freedom I feel is incredible." Her willingness to stretch actually revived her career. "I like going to work now because I am so happy."

Stretching comes easier when you stay focused on your Soul's purpose, your passion, doing what you love.

"Your BIGGEST gift to me was your admonition to stretch—to not run from being uncomfortable," wrote a retreat participant. "What I found is that being uncomfortable is no longer as uncomfortable. Disappointments and even outright refusals or rejections now feel like part of the landscape, instead of the monumental cliffs I had imagined them to be before."

The stretch that handicaps women most is their reluctance, or refusal, to ask for help. When I asked a successful businesswoman if, in hindsight, there was anything she'd do differently, her response was instantaneous. "Ask for help sooner," she replied. "When I had a big cash shortfall, I talked to experienced people. What was so humiliating and embarrassing to me was just typical growing pains of a successful business."

"No one does this alone," an executive told me. "If you try to, you won't grow."

"Success is a social activity," explained Karen Page, a prolific author I interviewed for another book. This is an important message in *Sacred Success*. Yet it tends to be a terrifying stretch for many women.

Have you noticed, in gyms, when guys are lifting really heavy weights, they ask someone, often a perfect stranger, to spot them? How many times have you seen a woman tap someone to watch her? Hardly ever! We'll hire trainers, but we'll rarely ask another for help, especially if we think the other person is "busy."

Why? Because we seldom lift very heavy weights; because we don't want to bother anyone; because we're determined to do it alone.

But as part of *Sacred Success*, we're required to lift heavier weights in order to build up our confidence, strengthen our resolve, and climb to greater heights. For this, we need our spotters, people we trust to have our backs, push us further, give us feedback.

The spotter's job is to:

1. Speak words of encouragement ("You can do it"). No negativity allowed.
2. Offer feedback for improvement.
3. Always conclude by saying: "Good work."

"Prior to *Sacred Success*," said insurance executive Erin, "I felt like I was the one that had to do everything. That philosophy had done me well for many years. We were in the top 25 percent of the agents in this area. But when I stopped thinking I had to do it all, I recognized I could use my team to support me in my mission, by doing only what I loved doing and delegating the rest to them."

Erin readily admits that delegating "was a foreign concept" to her. For many women like Erin, requesting support is both foreign and frightening, but something they quickly come to appreciate.

"Immediately our results skyrocketed," said Erin. "For the first time in five years, we were number one in our regional area, tied with another guy. We made significantly more money. And this next year will be even more dramatic." Then she added proudly, "And I'm only working two days a week!"

Teams factor high in *Sacred Success*. They not only enable businesses to grow exponentially, but also allow women to eventually earn more while working less. Almost every interview contained these words: "I worked harder at the beginning, but now I have a great team."

"There's a shift that occurs when you realize that as an individual you can only go so far," said one million-dollar earner. "To grow, you need a team."

This same sentiment was echoed by another high-level executive. "Doing grand things requires multiple people, teams for entrepreneurs and employees alike."

Here's how they effectively manage their teams for maximum performance:

- Find people with talents you don't have, not clones.
- Hire the best, and get out of their way.
- Set up systems, policies, and processes.
- Help others achieve their maximum potential.
- Stick with where you're most effective.
- Address problems immediately.

For many, managing teams figured prominently into their personal mission and fit well with their inclination to help others. "I feel what I do is part of something bigger, and bringing people along is part of that," said a business owner. "You grow by helping others." And still another declared, "People need a place to shine. I give it to them."

These women's teams, however, extended way beyond their job sites. Their teams included financial and legal advisors, coaches, colleagues, professional groups, and trusted friends. While men often figured prominently into their success, they all pointed to a cherished sisterhood that took them through the toughest of times. They consistently mentioned organizations like the Committee of 200, the International Women's Forum, or the Women Presidents' Organization, as being "the source of my sanity, priceless emotional support."

"These meetings," one woman explained, "nourished me to the core." Founder Marsha Firestone described the WPO as "women collaborating in a confidential environment with a commitment to be really supportive and helpful to each other."

Erin was longing for this kind of support team, so she invited a handful of businesswomen to a neighborhood restaurant. They've been meeting monthly for over a year.

"It's grown from eight women to thirty women attending on a regular basis," she told me. "I haven't done one ounce of marketing for it. But, apparently, women love what we're doing. They keep telling their friends, and it's growing. My list when I started was twelve people long and now it's well over sixty."

STEP 3: TOUGHEN UP.

"Pushy broad is one of the nicer names I've been called and I wear it as a badge of honor. While a few of my union brothers don't like me, they sure do respect me."

—Linda Chavez-Thompson, when she was executive vice president of the AFL

By nature, women tend to be pleasers. We want everyone to like us. Women making millions are no different. Almost everyone I interviewed confessed to a "little girl inside me who wants to be liked." But these women, like the rest of us, are frequently required to make difficult, even painful decisions that often have negative consequences for other people.

"You have to do the hard stuff," said one. That "hard stuff" includes those excruciating stretches such as ending relationships, firing employees, saying no, holding tight during demanding negotiations, enforcing an unpopular policy, dismissing high-paying but difficult clients, even enduring multiple rejections and disappointments.

Many of the women I interviewed regretted coming late to making tough decisions. "I didn't take off the velvet gloves soon enough. I kept trying to be nice," one woman sighed. "Eventually I had to toughen up."

When I share this insight with women in my retreat, I see many smile knowingly, but uneasily. As executive assistant Julie Anne quipped, only partly joking, "You mean I can say what I think, feel, and want, and nobody dies? Who knew?"

Victoria Edwards, the advertising executive, recalled, "All my life I've worked incredibly hard to make everyone comfortable at my own expense, in love, in life, in work. As things get uncomfortable, I swoop in and make it better—always. I am making a promise to myself here and now that I will never go back to that heads-down, work-hard, ask-for-nothing-in-return victim mentality!"

When Victoria returned home from our retreat, she was offered a job with another company. She knew she had to toughen up to negotiate a higher salary and equity in the company. Victoria was actually surprised at how powerful she felt and how effective she was when she stood tall and spoke her truth.

"I let them know that it would take considerably more than they were offering to get me to leave my current job and take on the risk of working at a small private company," she declared proudly. "The CEO and president said they would never give me equity in their company." She stuck to her guns though it was incredibly unnerving.

"It worked," she proclaimed. "They saw me as the exec they wanted. I was standing up for my needs, so they knew I could stand up for theirs.

When we left that night, both of them hugged me, and the next day before I could write a thank-you note, the CEO emailed me that they were giving me equity in the company and they'd be sending me a revised offer."

Victoria admitted this was a first. "I never used to ask for what I wanted and I always overworked, but now, even in my current job, I am working 60 percent less and 100 percent smarter and it is paying off," she exclaimed.

A few days later, she had another chance to toughen up when she got a "public berating" from her current boss—not for the first time. This time, however, she opted to stretch by standing up for herself.

"I will never tolerate that from a boss again," she declared with a tinge of surprise and a heaping dose of confidence. "It was so awesome to hear my voice standing up for me and all others in that room that had taken his abuse. Actually, I think he respected me for it."

"Toughening up" doesn't mean you have to harden your heart, numb your senses, or act all macho. "Toughness doesn't have to come in a pinstripe suit," explained Senator Dianne Feinstein.

"Toughening up" *does* require a dramatic shift in mind-set, which sounds like this: *I'd rather be respected than liked.* I heard this same line from virtually every ultra–high earner I interviewed. "I tried to be nice rather than stand by my convictions," one woman told me. "Then I learned you can't always be liked, but you can definitely be respected."

The recognition that earning respect is more important than gaining approval was for many a "watershed moment." It's what allows us, as women, to be powerful without being punitive, forthright without being unfeeling, responsible without being ruthless, to develop a "rhinoceros' hide" while keeping an open heart, and to become confident leaders without compromising our femininity.

"Since *Sacred Success*, I've gotten a lot better at having those harder conversations that in the past would have felt so confrontational and I would've avoided at all cost," Suzy Carroll said. "I find if I set my intention before a conversation, it goes well."

For example, an employee was all set to purchase Suzy's store—until, she said, "it hit me from every angle that I did not want to sell. That meant I had to sit down and have a tough conversation with her. I didn't want her to leave because I'd invested so much in training her. I also really enjoy having her there. So I was nervous. But it was amazing."

Before the meeting, Suzy meditated briefly. "I set my intention that I would speak from my heart, and that the words that came out would be supportive and good for both of us. And that is exactly how the meeting went. She was actually relieved. I had no idea. The whole meeting I was guided by my Soul."

True, toughness is required in many situations. But because we are so relationship-oriented, we also need a place where we can let our hair down and be ourselves. I noticed that successful women all had what I call a "Love Nest." I highly recommend you find yours. A love nest is comprised of family, friends, and loved ones who provide a safe place where you can be a scared, insecure little girl and they'll listen empathetically, encourage you wholeheartedly, and accept you unconditionally. Sometimes our spotters are part of our love nest, but not always.

EXERCISE: Who's in Your Love Nest?

List the names of people in your life who you can be totally yourself with. When you're feeling vulnerable, scared, insecure, or just plain awful, contact someone on this list to love you up.

STEP 4: THINK STRATEGICALLY.

"Keep your eyes on the stars, your feet on the ground."

—*Franklin D. Roosevelt*

Strategic thinking means keeping one eye on your higher purpose without taking the other eye off the bottom line. Perhaps it's their background in sports, or their access to senior-level mentors, that makes men savvier about thinking strategically. Women, in their eagerness to give back to their community, or give birth to their dreams, often neglect this critical step.

To think strategically, you must constantly link the big picture to the costs of doing business, or to put it another way, connect your purpose statement to your profit/loss statement. By the way, this step also applies to those who don't run a business, manage a department, or even work for remuneration. *Sacred Success* insists that you think strategically about your personal finances (we'll talk more about this in Chapter 7), keeping one eye on your daily endeavors and the other on your checkbook balance.

"The secret to a million dollars is continuously reevaluating the expenses to run a lean, mean business," said a business owner. "Once you know where the profit is, it's just a matter of multiplying how many widgets you need to sell."

A senior vice president explained it this way: "Connect everything with the numbers. To be a successful businesswoman, you have to strategize all the time on how to make the numbers work."

Strategic thinking involves:

- Figuring out the costs of doing business
- Creating a plan to keep costs low and revenues growing
- Cutting losses when something isn't working
- Designing effective structures and systems

- Integrating data and new information
- Daily/monthly strategizing and yearly long-term planning

Strategic thinking did not come easily to many of the women I interviewed. "This is not my nature," said a former newspaper reporter. "I'm a writer. It was something I had to learn. No matter how passionate you are, you have to have business savvy."

Fortunately, you can learn to think strategically by reading books, taking classes, talking to others, joining peer groups, forming an advisory team, seeking out mentors, consulting with professionals in or outside your industry.

Here's another place where Discipline and Surrender do-si-do. Strategic thinking requires small doses of Surrender, short periods of uninterrupted downtime. A *Fast Company* article about LinkedIn CEO Jeff Weiner noted that he scheduled thirty- to ninety-minute blocks of time for strategic thinking.

"Think about what the company will look like in three to five years," Weiner wrote on his blog. "Think about the best way to improve an already popular product or address an unmet customer need; think about how you can widen a competitive advantage or close a competitive gap, etc."

One of the exercises we do in the *Sacred Success* retreat is form a four-person strategic task force. You can do this at home. Invite people you trust, respect, and admire. Meet with them regularly to help you stay on track strategically, or contact them when you need tactical solutions to problematic situations.

EXERCISE: Assemble a Strategic Task Force

Think of a stretch you need/want to take. Describe it to your group. Ask them for advice, feedback, comments, or suggestions. Then listen and jot down what they tell you. The only rule: You cannot say "Yes, but . . ." Whatever the others suggest, stay open, take notes, and say thank you.

When Victoria negotiated her new executive job, she said, "I received advice from not only my strategic task force during the retreat, which was so helpful. I reached out to my boyfriend, who helped me from a small-business perspective, and my job coach. I got a huge realization that if a negotiation is uncomfortable—you're doing it right!"

The Magic of Small Steps

> *"You don't start out thinking I'm going to be a star. You think I hope I get an agent. Then I hope I get an audition. Then I hope I get a call back. Then I hope I get a job. If you think too far ahead, it's just overwhelming. It's better to just keep on going bit by bit, one foot in front of the other."*
>
> —Julianne Moore

Discipline is the art of putting one foot in front of the other, doing what you need to do to achieve your aims, even if it's not what you *want* to do. Discipline is much easier to sustain when you travel in small steps, accomplishing tiny, short-term goals while pursuing your Soul's larger purpose.

As rock musician Luci described it, "It's about keeping my immediate goal clear, and simultaneously feeling the thrill when visualizing the really big vision. But I don't have to plan all the little stepping-stones. This kind of thinking gets me crazy in the head because the answers aren't there and won't be until I accomplish the immediate goal. And then the next immediate goal. So simple!"

I laughed so hard when I heard from investment advisor, author, and self-proclaimed workaholic Manisha Thakor months after the retreat. "Change is so funny," she wrote, "It can feel like you are making no progress at all yet so long as you keep putting one foot in front of the other, even it if it's just an inch . . . WHAM—next thing you know you've set a goal of taking eight to ten weeks of vacation a year and you spend your first three weeks of that time in Laos. Next up, Finland,

Germany, and at some point Argentina. Truly cannot thank you enough for encouraging me to quite literally 'get a life.'"

Discipline, in partnership with Surrender, gives you enormous power. But there's a specific type of Disciplined Action that you need to understand—the Discipline of Affluence—before you're ready for the fourth and final stage of *Sacred Success*. This Discipline is compulsory to complete your passage to power. Breathe easy—it's much less complicated and more enjoyable than you may expect.

CHAPTER SUMMARY: Disciplined Action—Stage 3

- Disciplined Action—consistent activity in the direction of your desire—operates in tandem with Receptive Surrender.

- Disciplined Action means *doing with discernment*, thoughtfully pruning rather than tirelessly pushing.

- Discipline comes from the Latin word *discipul*, meaning "*being a disciple unto oneself.*"

- Disciplined Action stems from Disciplined Thinking, focusing on your strengths and your value while denying the Ego's lies about your inadequacy.

- The exhilarating secret of Disciplined Action: Fear fades with action.

- Be wary of falling into scattered, frantic, or random activity. Busyness is the absence of discipline.

- Four Steps to Disciplined Action:

  ○ Step 1: Ask yourself: How will I pursue my purpose?

  ○ Step 2: Comply with the Law of Growth.

  ○ Step 3: Toughen up.

  ○ Step 4: Think strategically.

STAGE 3 HOMEWORK

EXERCISE: Values Clarification

Below is a list of values. Circle the ten that are most important to you. If you don't see an important value on this list, add it. Give yourself time to really explore and think about these.

Acceptance	Fun	Leadership	Simplicity
Achievement	Generosity	Learning	Sisterhood
Adventure	God	Leaving a legacy	Spirituality
Aging well	Growth	Leisure	Strength
Beauty	Happiness	Life partner	Success
Charity	Harmony	Love	Support
Comfort	Health	Making a difference	Surrender
Commitment	Honesty	Parenting	Time alone
Communication	Honor	Patriotism	Transformation
Community	Humility	Peace	Truth
Courage	Independence	Physical activity	Using my talents
Creativity	Individuality	Power	Wisdom
Democracy	Influence	Respect	Others
Dignity	Inner peace	Responsibility	
Discovery	Integrity	Retirement	
Diversity	Intimacy	Security	
Education	Joy	Seeing the world	
Family	Justice	Self-discipline	
Freedom	Kindness	Self-esteem	
Friendship	Knowledge	Service	

Next, cross out five that you circled and rank the five that remain in order of importance.

My Most Important Values

1.

2.

3.

4.

5.

Now that you know what values are most important to you, from this point on, before making any decisions, before saying YES or NO to anything, ask yourself this question:

Will this get me closer, or take me further, from my values, from pursuing my highest purpose, living my deepest truths?

TEN SIGNS OF DISCIPLINED ACTION

Use these ten signs as a daily checklist. Put a copy where you'll see it, and every evening, go through each item, checking off the ones you followed. My bet—this simple exercise will have you disciplined in no time!

1. I know what I want and am committed to getting it. (And if I don't know, I devote time and energy to figuring it out.)

2. I am so focused on my vision that I don't get distracted or scattered by irrelevant, draining, or conflicting tasks.

3. I am willing to experience whatever it takes—defeat, embarrassment, even humiliation—to achieve what I want.

4. I am always doing things I've never done before and/or don't want to do.

5. I make at least one unreasonable (i.e., scary) request of others a week.

6. I don't say "yes" when I really want to say "no," even if it means rocking the boat or upsetting another person.

7. I regularly seek support, and refuse to spend time with or discuss my dream with naysayers (even if they're part of my family).

8. Every time I'm afraid to do something, I force myself to do it anyway. (And I catch myself when I try to justify not doing it.)

9. I am rigorous about what I think and the words I speak, making sure they're positive, supportive, and appreciative (of myself and others).

10. I take time to relax and pamper myself so I don't burn out.

CHAPTER 6

Disciplined Action, Part 2— The Discipline of Affluence

"Nothing you understand is fearful."

—A Course in Miracles

Let's Talk about Money, Shall We?

"Money which represents the prose of life and which is hardly spoken of in parlors without an apology, is in its effects and laws, as beautiful as roses."

—Ralph Waldo Emerson

Before we go any farther, there's someone I'd like you to meet—your *Inner Financier*. If you didn't know you had an *Inner Financier*, it's high time you got acquainted. I expect you will become fast friends.

There's a phenomenon that occurs when a woman finally connects with her *Inner Financier*. Maybe you know what I'm talking about. She feels radically different, as if she's been initiated into a secret society of sacred knowledge, or emerged from a dark cave into the dazzling light of clarity and competence. At some point, when this happens, she will inevitably utter the following words: "I feel so powerful."

I can tell you, it's an exhilarating feeling, the ultimate high, to realize that by taking charge of your money, you're taking charge of your life. The sense of power this brings is very real, indescribably delicious, and life altering. Your *Inner Financier* is indispensable for your passage from a dependent child to an autonomous adult. But as you'd probably guess, your Ego is no fan of your *Inner Financier* and will try mightily to come between you. It takes scrupulous discipline to stay in contact with her, especially at the outset of your relationship.

I suspect, for some of you, pairing money with discipline is a definite turnoff. In fact, you're probably tempted to skip this chapter altogether. I urge you to keep reading. As I've said repeatedly, the quickest way to diminish your power (along with your confidence) is by ignoring your money. Believe me, you'll never reach Greatness if your money is sitting unattended, or worse yet, a total mess. Let me explain why.

There are three levels of financial development:

Level 1: Survival (*not enough*)—doing whatever it takes to stay afloat.
Level 2: Stability (*enough*)—generating sufficient cash flow to meet your needs, eliminate debt, and protect your future.
Level 3: Affluence (*more than enough*)—accumulating ample disposable income that allows you to live life on your own terms.

There are basically three ways to obtain affluence: inherit it, marry it, or earn it. I lucked out on the first, have given up on the second, and am delightfully working on the third.

As I've experienced, the game changes considerably when you move into Level 2. Free from the stress of *not enough*, you can now lay the foundation for *Sacred Success*. But until you grasp the Discipline of Affluence, you won't be in any shape to heartily tackle Stage 4, which is where the power, and the fun, reside.

There are actually two kinds of affluent women—the Powerful Affluent and the Precarious Affluent. Most women fall into the second category, where money—no matter how much they have—is a source of stress, anxiety, and pain. In the first category, money serves as a powerful tool for pleasure, healing, and transformation.

"Money in the bank makes life so much easier," said a top-level executive.

"I believe economic security is the keystone to a meaningful life," said another.

Becoming a Powerful Affluent requires Disciplined Action: setting financial boundaries, making scary decisions, stretching by taking well-considered risks, strategizing about how to make your money grow. If your net worth isn't growing, it's shrinking. And, metaphorically, so are you.

This is something Victoria Trabosh, life coach and philanthropist, learned when she finally eliminated her debt and increased her savings by $40,000: "I've been playing small by not managing my money. I don't think I really respected money. I feared it."

The Discipline of Affluence is all about respecting money. But above all, it's about respecting yourself.

It's a Matter of Mind-Set

> "We buy things we don't need with money we don't
> have to impress people we don't like."
>
> —Dave Ramsey

More than anything, becoming a Powerful Affluent by managing your money requires mental discipline. Regardless of how much you make, what matters most is your mind-set. In other words, do you think like a *Consumer* or a *Wealth Builder*? There *is* a major difference between the two. The Consumer is Ego based. The Wealth Builder (otherwise known as your *Inner Financier*) is sourced from your Soul.

A Consumer thinks: "I want more money so I can buy more clothes, take more trips, eat out more often, and have more fun."

The Wealth Builder thinks: "I want more money to save and invest for the long term so that I can have more ease, more freedom, more choices, and more opportunities to help others."

Do you know what separates these mind-sets? *Instant gratification.* It's the difference between snapping up those Prada shoes—which you simply *must have* because they go perfectly with that Juicy Couture dress you just bought—or depositing that same sum straight into a mutual fund. The decision is yours to make.

I'm not suggesting self-deprivation. There's a world of difference between denial and discipline. True, the discipline of saving may require *delayed gratification.* But think of it this way—you're giving the money to *YOU* (not MasterCard) so that ultimately you can purchase what you please without pressure or worry.

Climb Aboard the Wealth-Builder Wagon

> *"Beloved, I wish above all things that thou mayest prosper."*
>
> *—3 John 1:2*

We all know how to be a Consumer. It's easy. Money comes in. We go out and spend it. No discipline required. Wealth Building, on the other hand, *seems* complicated. But that's because no one ever taught us the Discipline of Affluence.

The truth is:

- Wealth Building is a lot simpler than you think.
- It doesn't take a lot of time to get smart.
- It doesn't take a lot of money to create wealth.
- It's never too late to begin.

Once you climb on the Wealth-Builder wagon, life looks a whole lot brighter and feels much less stressful. I'm speaking from experience. The secret to building wealth is simply this: *Wealth doesn't come from what you have. Wealth comes from what you DO with what you have.* Look at all the highly paid celebrities and athletes who've gone bankrupt. Essentially, you build wealth by following what I call the **Four Rules of Money**, each one a Disciplined Action in itself.

1. *Spend Less*—never spend money you don't have. If you can't pay off your credit cards in full each month, stop using them.

2. *Save More*—pay yourself first. Ideally, 10 percent of every dollar goes straight into savings. If you can only afford ten dollars a month, that's fine. Have it automatically transferred monthly into a separate account.

3. *Invest Wisely*—put at least a portion of your money into assets that have the potential to outpace inflation.

4. *Give Generously*—no explanation needed here. Most of us have the giving generously part down pat.

Important warning: These rules must be followed in this order. Giving without adhering to the first three rules is an act of self-sabotage. Not only do you jeopardize your future security; you also diminish your capacity to fully engage in the final stage.

While each of the Four Rules of Money is important, Investing Wisely is the one that throws most women off the Wealth-Builder wagon. The problem is that learning about investing can feel like climbing Kilimanjaro—intimidating, daunting, even downright impossible. Actually, I suspect some of you would rather take on the mountain than tackle the stock market.

Perhaps you're thinking, "I understand why I need to spend less and save more. But in these crazy times, wouldn't it be infinitely safer and simpler to just keep my money in a jam jar? Why even bother with investing?"

It's true. The economy *is* crazy. The markets *are* unpredictable. But if there's a lesson to be learned from the Great Recession, it's this: *Never confuse safety with ignorance.* This is not a time to ignore money and pretend everything will be okay. That's partly what got our world into this mess in the first place—banks wearing blinders, lending money to people buying houses they couldn't afford; supposedly smart people, industry insiders, buying "toxic" derivatives they didn't understand, fudging the rules or blatantly ignoring them. Complacency without comprehension is supremely dangerous.

So right now, let's take our own blinders off. We'll begin with a question from your *Inner Financier.* It's an important question, so I want you to really think about the answer. *What is the biggest financial risk to you as a woman?* (Hint: It's not the market crashing.) Your biggest risk—because we live longer than men—is that you will outlive your money, that your savings will not grow as fast as inflation and taxes will take it away. Stuffing your entire life savings in a dresser drawer is like living in a house full of termites. Even if nothing seems awry, you'll doubtlessly be dealing with costly damages down the line.

Wealth Building 101

> *"The trick is to make sure you don't die waiting for prosperity to happen."*
>
> —Lee Iacocca

So, in our quest to make informed financial decisions, your *Inner Financier* is going to demystify Wealth Building by breaking it into its most basic building blocks, its lowest common denominators.

We've spent much of this book concentrating on the psychological, spiritual, and emotional aspects of success. But now we're acknowledging that a basic understanding of money management is vital to *Sacred*

Success. Your *Inner Financier* has been patiently waiting to give her crash course on using money to make money. Perhaps you'll have a similar epiphany as the filmmaker who blurted out, "Oh my God, I just realized I'm working way harder for my money than it's been working for me." Call it "Investing Made Simple—very, *very* simple!"

Whenever money comes to you, you have two options. You can do what Consumers do and give it all to Nordstrom, Target, Starbucks, the slots, your kids, etc. The list is endless. Or you can become a Wealth Builder by putting at least part of your income to work in places that will, over time, grow at a faster clip than the rate of inflation.

In the first option, you're waving bye-bye to your bank balance. In the second, you're watching your money earn even more money, which you can judiciously and joyfully give to American Express, Macy's, or your favorite charities without losing a wink of sleep. So, let's start simplifying investing. Welcome to **Wealth Building 101** in nine simple lessons.

Wealth-Building Lesson 1

> *"The wise man saves for the future but the foolish man spends whatever he gets."*
>
> —Proverbs 21:20

The good news is that the list of places to invest, or build wealth, is *not* endless. In fact, the number is quite limited. There are only five places to invest money, otherwise known as asset classes. The five asset classes are:

1. Stocks
2. Bonds
3. Real estate
4. Cash
5. Commodities

That's it! Only five categories you need to understand.

Wealth-Building Lesson 2

*"It is better to tell your money where to go than
wonder where it went."*

—Unknown

Things get even simpler. These five asset classes fall into only two categories. What that means: There are only two different ways to invest. You
either (1) own or (2) loan. Let's look at each asset class and try guessing
which ones you own and which ones you loan.

Stocks—Take a guess. If you said "Own," you're right. When Company X wants to raise money, it sells shares in an initial public offering (IPO). Companies that sell stock to shareholders are called
public companies. When you buy shares in Company X, you, the
shareholder, actually own a piece of the company. If Company X
makes money, so do you. Of course, the opposite is true too.

Bonds—*Own* or *loan?* The answer: *Loan.* Another way that an
organization—a company, municipality, or government—raises
money is to ask the public for a loan. They promise to pay you, the
lender or bondholder, back in full at the agreed-upon time, and also
pay you interest on the loan.

Real estate—*Own* or *loan?* Okay, this one's easy: *Own.* You buy
houses, apartments, office buildings, or raw land. Real estate has
made people rich. But there's no guarantee, as we've seen with the
last housing bust. Also, an important drawback is that real estate is
not very liquid. In other words, you can't readily convert your home
to cash because it usually takes time to sell. Here's where I want to

make an important distinction between your home and say, a rental property. Technically, I don't count *my own house* as an investment. Even though, hopefully, its value is going up, I don't want to have to sell it if I need money.

Cash—This one's a bit tricky: *Loan*. Unless all your money is tucked away in a hiding place at home, you actually lend it to the bank when you open an account. In return, the bank promises to pay you interest, otherwise known as *yield*. Cash also includes "cash equivalents" such as CDs (certificates of deposit), treasuries, and money market funds.

Commodities—I'll make this easy: *Own*. These are tangible products, like pork bellies, wheat, gold, oil, and silver, which are traded (bought or sold) on various commodities exchanges. There's an old joke: "How do you make a small fortune in commodities? Start with a large one." Commodities are extremely risky, so unless you're very rich and work with a pro, you probably shouldn't be investing in them.

Wealth-Building Lesson 3

"It's only too late if you don't start now."

—*Barbara Sher*

As I pointed out earlier, keeping all your money in cash, or under the mattress for that matter, may seem simpler and safer, but over time, it's extremely hazardous to your financial health. Remember, our biggest risk is outliving our money due to inflation and taxes. Inflation is like the hungry little caterpillar in the children's book, that instead of leaves, keeps nibbling away at our money until after a while there's hardly anything left. Consider this: Since 1926,

- inflation has averaged 3 percent annually,
- cash has returned about 3 percent annually (though as of this writing, the returns are pretty paltry),
- stocks have grown about 10 percent annually,
- bonds return about 5 percent annually, and
- real estate has grown about 6.2 percent annually.

Wealth-Building Lesson 4

"I have enough money to last me the rest of my life, unless I need to buy something."

—*Jackie Mason*

Now's a good time to explain the *Rule of 72*. This rule lets you figure out how many years it'll take to double your money. Here's how it works: Divide the interest rate (the percentage of the loan that a borrower pays to the lender) or compounded return (the accumulated return when interest paid on the original amount also earns interest) into the number seventy-two. For example, let's say you invest in a mutual fund that returns about 8 percent annually. Eight divided into seventy-two is nine. It will take nine years to double your initial investment.

If all your money is sitting in the bank, paying at best 3 percent interest, you'll need twenty-four years to see it double. Can you see the risk you take by only investing in cash?

Wealth-Building Lesson 5

"Knowing how to do something and doing it are two different things."

—*Casey Stengel*

Let's talk about one of my favorite subjects—risk, a word that, when used in the same sentence as money, used to scare me silly. The dictionary defines risk as *the possibility of suffering harm or loss*. That's how I always regarded investing, as a guarantee of losing all my money. After all, my ex-husband had blown my inheritance playing the market.

I swore I'd never get involved in such a dicey endeavor ever again. But then I interviewed women who were smart about money. They had a vastly different take on risk. To them, risk provided the opportunity for gain.

It's worth repeating: *Risk provides the opportunity for gain*. In the market, risk is linked to *volatility*. Prices go up; prices go down. But *price swings* only matter when you *sell*. Everything else is just noise. You know—the sound of the market doing what markets are supposed to do: up/down/up/down—boing/boing/boing. The discipline required here is to turn a deaf ear to erratic fluctuations since you're investing for the long term (more about this in Lesson 6).

Let's take a look at the stock market during an average twenty-year period:

Okay, it's not scientifically accurate, but you get the gist. The market looks just like a roller coaster, right? But notice anything else? The trajectory has consistently been up. Here's what I want you to remember: *It's the overall direction, not the day-to-day bouncing that matters*. Volatility is unavoidable. But a market in flux doesn't guarantee loss. It holds the possibility for profit.

As esteemed financial writer Jane Bryant Quinn once said: "It's a fact. Stock investors sometimes lose money on their way to wealth. Get over it."

Investments go down. That's a fact. Volatility happens. Get over it. Rather than panic, understand how to stack the odds in your favor. You can minimize your risk of loss significantly. There are two ways, and I'll explain both.

Wealth-Building Lesson 6

"It's possible to have risk (a good thing) without debilitating fear or its best friend, obsessive worry."

—Seth Godin

One way to diminish risk is by understanding how "Time" (not "Timing") works. Remember that markets function like roller coasters. They go up; they go down. It's all part of the fun. It's also why some really smart people were suspicious of Bernie Madoff, the guy who pulled off probably the largest investment scam in history. His returns never went down. They were consistently positive. A few clever folks saw this as a glaring red flag. All investments go down on occasion. Some do so more frequently and more severely than others, but even the very best will take some tumbles.

Remember, market gyrations only matter when you sell your holdings. It's called the Rule of the Roller Coaster (borrowed from the late broadcaster Paul Harvey): *The only one who gets hurt riding a roller coaster is the one who jumps off.*

When people try to time the market—buying when they're sure it's headed higher, or selling because they suspect it's about to plummet—that's not investing; that's gambling. Trying to predict the markets is like rolling the dice at the craps tables. Countless people have tried and failed. A few luck out, but rarely consistently.

The truth is, no one knows what the market is going to do, except that it will go down and it'll go up. So here's the big secret to stacking the odds in your favor: *Respect the time factor.* What do I mean by that?

- Money you'll need in 1–3 years—put into cash.
- Money you'll need in 3–10 years—put into stocks, bonds, and cash.
- Money you'll need in 10+ years—put into stocks, real estate, and commodities.

If you don't know when you'll need the money, err on the safe side. Invest your cash in liquid assets, like cash, stocks, or bonds that are easy to sell, unlike real estate and commodities.

A PAINFUL LESSON

> *"All things, events, encounters and circumstances are helpful."*
>
> —A Course in Miracles

I learned this lesson the hard way. After my first divorce in 1986, I invested a small amount with a broker. He'd constantly send me statements that I didn't understand, so I threw them away. A year later, in October 1987, the market crashed, big time. I freaked out, called my broker, told him to sell everything. He begged me to stay put.

"The market will go back up," he said. "It always does, and if you sell now you're going to have capital gains to pay." I had no idea what capital gains were. I just wanted my money where it was "safe." Of course, the market rebounded, very quickly. If I had understood then about the time factor, I'd be a lot richer now. But I got the message: Don't even try to time the market.

Fast forward, ten years later—October 1997—almost to the day. The market crashed again. My book *Prince Charming Isn't Coming* had just been published. I knew a lot more about investing by then. This time I was on the phone first thing in the morning, calling my advisor. My now second ex-husband was upstairs, pacing the floor. He would get very nervous whenever the market went south. My teenage daughter came downstairs, saw me on the phone, and asked me what I was doing.

"I'm buying stock," I told her.

"But Mom, the market's crashing."

"No, Anna," I said, "it's a sale!"

Finally, I understood how things worked. I knew that eventually the market would go back up. I didn't know when, but I knew it would. And right at that moment stock prices were bargains. I was buying good companies that weren't about to go under. And I was investing money I knew I wouldn't need for at least ten years.

Wealth-Building Lesson 7

"Three-fifths of all lottery winners file for bankruptcy in three years."

—*Money (magazine)*

My first foray into the market taught me another big lesson. I call it the First Law of Investing: *Never invest in anything you don't understand,* whether it's a stock or bond or the market itself. Not only don't you understand what you're buying, but you aren't able to properly evaluate information to know when to sell.

Wealth-Building Lesson 8

"Take away my twelve best investments and my portfolio is mediocre at best."

—*Warren Buffett*

The second way to minimize risk of loss when investing is through diversification, or putting your eggs/money in a lot of different baskets. Each of the five asset classes are individual baskets: stocks, bonds, real estate, cash, and commodities. Moreover, every asset class can be further divided into subclasses. For example:

- Stocks can be classified by size: small, medium, and large company stocks (otherwise known as small-, medium-, and large-*cap* stocks).

- Bonds can be classified by type: corporate, municipal, and government bonds.

- Regional stocks/bonds can be classified by geography: US, overseas, and emerging markets.

Each of these different asset classes, or subclasses, reacts differently to various conditions and time periods. So when, say, small-cap stocks take a hit, large companies may be doing great. Or when US stocks are tanking, European companies may be holding their own, and emerging markets may be soaring.

It doesn't always work that way. Sometimes a turbulent sea sinks all ships. But for the most part, diversification protects your overall holdings. And since you never know what sector will take the next beating, diversification reduces the volatility of your whole portfolio. In fact, studies indicate that diversification accounts for 93 percent of a portfolio's overall performance. Only 2 percent comes from stock picking, and 3 percent from luck.

Only 2 percent from picking the right stock! We make ourselves crazy trying to find the best companies, when we should be putting more energy into making sure we're sensibly spread out over numerous categories.

THE CASE FOR MUTUAL FUNDS

> *"Trying to pick the best stocks is like expecting to hit the apple with the first arrow."*
>
> *—Kiplinger's Personal Finance*

One way to diversify is to purchase a whole bunch of individual equities. The problem, however, is this can be expensive. You need a lot of money to buy enough shares of enough companies, or enough individual bonds, to be diversified. A fatal mistake that people frequently make is putting all their money into a single holding, such as their company stock. Now *that* is *really* risky. We saw what happened, years ago, to all those who put their entire retirement in WorldCom or Enron. Both were superb companies that eventually went belly-up. A good rule of thumb for investing: *Never put any money in any one single investment that you can't afford to lose.*

That's why mutual funds have become so popular. Mutual funds are baskets, or containers, that hold a bunch of different individual equities, or various combinations of stocks, bonds, commodities, and even real estate. Each fund is managed by an individual or a team of experts in their field, who are presumably a lot smarter than you and me. After all, that's what they do all day—study the assets they're trading. (There are exceptions, such as index funds, where a fund is not managed by a person but mimics a market, such as the S&P or the Dow Industrials.) When you buy shares in a fund, your money is pooled with other folks who also bought shares in the fund. You own a slice of all the stocks combined. The size of your slice depends on how many shares you purchase.

There is a lot to learn about mutual funds, but let's stick to what I call the Big Four. These are among the most important factors to understand when buying, or selling, a fund.

1. **Fees.** All funds have fees. There are *load funds*, which charge a sales fee. And there are *no load funds* that don't. But all funds, even no loads, charge something, including management fees, marketing fees, distributions fees, and so on. These fees—which range from less than 0.10 percent to more than 2.00 percent—are deducted from your net returns. I'm a fan of low fees. But if you're paying high fees, your fund better be performing way above average to make up for the costs they're taking out.

2. **History.** In selecting a fund, you want to look at its performance history over a three-year, five-year, and ten-year period; how it's

done in up markets and down; and its value before tax and after tax returns. Resist the temptation to buy the hottest fund of the day. Funds, like hemlines, go in and out of fashion. I can almost guarantee that this year's number one performer will be among next year's biggest duds.

3. **Changes.** You need to know if there have been any recent changes to the fund, especially in management, the people who make the investment decisions. When the manager changes, that can, though it doesn't have to, affect a fund's performance. Also, keep an eye out for any changes in the fund's objectives. For example, you originally bought a small-cap fund, but its holdings have grown, and now it's made up mostly of mid- and large-cap companies. These changes can make a big difference in the fund's performance and throw your diversification plan off kilter.

4. **Comparables.** To fully evaluate a fund, always check to see how the fund's performance compares with other funds in its category, as well as how it has compared over time. It may seem like a fund is doing well, but compared with others it may be performing near the bottom. And if its fees are higher, that's a double red flag.

This is a lot to be aware of, which is why I work with a financial advisor (Lesson 9 below). However, you need to know what your advisor is recommending so that you can make informed decisions. Another good place to learn more about mutual funds is at Morningstar.com. Morningstar is a popular research firm that publishes reports, articles, and all kinds of valuable information about mutual funds, some of it free, some for a fee.

Wealth-Building Lesson 9

"Discipline is doing what doesn't come naturally."

—*Gary Renard*

Now, let's talk about *how* you invest. Your *Inner Financier* is eager to introduce you to the Investing Pyramid. When I first learned about this pyramid, it was like a huge lightbulb went on in my head. Here is my story:

After selling everything in the 1987 October crash, my first excursion back into the market was to purchase a limited partnership. The company, T.J. Cinnamons, sold sticky buns in shopping centers. I had no idea what a limited partnership was, but my father's friend, who was very smart, successful, and wealthy, had started the company. I totally trusted him, so I gave him some money. Big mistake. Remember, the First Law of Investing says *"never invest in anything you don't understand."* I knew what a sticky bun was, but I didn't understand that a limited partnership is totally *illiquid*. I couldn't sell my shares if I wanted to. When the company went bust, I lost everything I'd put in.

Fortunately, my investment was a small enough sum that it didn't wipe me out. Soon after, I was telling a CPA my tale of woe. He whipped out a piece of paper, drew a triangle, and explained that the best investment strategy is based on the traditional upright pyramid. You start at the bottom and work your way up, level by level. My mistake was that I had started at the top. Then he drew an upside-down pyramid, resting on its narrow tip. "See what happens when you start at the top?" he explained. "Your portfolio is not very stable, is it?" Suddenly the whole topic of investing made sense!

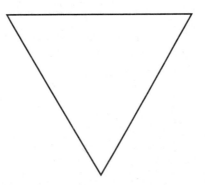

This pyramid represents the whole world of investing. Here, just as in investing, we'll start at the bottom and work our way up.

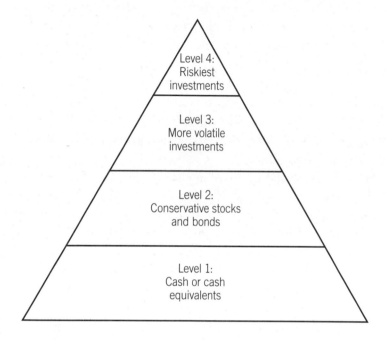

Level 1: Cash or cash equivalents. I call this your "Sleep at Night Money." There's little volatility at this level, so you're not likely to lose sleep worrying about loss. The first level includes CDs, treasuries, money market funds, and basic bank accounts. This level is your safety net. In case something happens, like losing your job or totaling your car, you've got cash to cover the unexpected. Otherwise, you'd be forced to accumulate debt.

How much should you keep in cash? Opinions vary. I sock away at least six to twelve months of living expenses in a cash reserve. I call this my "Untouchable Account." It's for emergencies only. I also have a "Touchable Account," where I put aside cash for a to-die-for designer sale or an I-gotta-get-away tropical vacation.

Investments at this level are the most stable, but, like all investments, they still carry risk. The risk here is inflation and taxes. Money in cash is like a wool sweater in a hot dryer, guaranteed to shrink over time.

Level 2: Conservative stocks and bonds. This is your "Inflation-Fighting Money." At least a portion of your portfolio needs to grow faster than inflation. This level fluctuates more than, say, treasuries. But the returns are still high enough to keep you ahead of inflation. Level 2 includes big, solid companies, higher-rated bonds (anything A-rated or higher), and mutual funds with a good track record. These investments are very liquid, which means your money can be converted to cash easily whenever you need it.

If you haven't already, make sure to invest in a tax-deferred retirement account: an IRA, Roth IRA, 401(k), or 403(b). Retirement accounts are gifts from the government gods (who don't give us many gifts); money invested in a retirement account is allowed to grow tax free. Ideally, you want to contribute as much as your employer or the government will allow, or at least put in as much as you possibly can every year. (Depending on your age, your retirement account may fall under Level 2 and Level 3.)

You also want to invest outside your retirement. But keep in mind, any money you'll need in the next three years—whether for a down payment on a house or your kid going to college—should stay in Level 1: Cash. The risk at this level is that you'll have to sell your holdings when the market is down and suffer a loss. That's why you need a longer time frame.

Level 3: More volatile investments. I call these your "Pack a Punch" investments. They include emerging markets, foreign funds, and junk bonds. The ride is much bumpier at this level. Price swings can be unrelenting and extreme. But these babies can sure ratchet up your returns. I have some in my portfolio, though they make up a much smaller percentage than my Level 2 holdings. The risk here is that these investments have much higher levels of volatility, so you will need a strong stomach and an even longer time frame.

Level 4: Riskiest investments. I affectionately call these the "Wild Ones." They include limited partnerships, venture capital, hedge funds, derivatives, options, and commodities. Investments at this level are particularly perilous. Gains can be enormous, but so can the losses. If you invest money here, you need nerves of steel and wads of cash. People at this level have made huge fortunes and have also been forced into bankruptcy. I rarely invest here because, frankly, I don't understand most of what's offered.

Entrepreneurs, guess which level an investment in your own business is in? Even if your company is not a start-up, it belongs in the very tippy top. I get very concerned when women tell me their largest, and sometimes their sole, investment is in their own firms. This is often how debt starts and ultimately spirals out of control. I urge women at my retreats to make sure they have a solid foundation of cash in the bank and a healthy retirement fund *before* they plough capital into their own companies.

Wealth-Building Lesson 9

"None of us is as smart as all of us."

—Ken Blanchard

I'm a big fan of working with financial professionals. You wouldn't fill your own cavities or set your own broken bone, would you? You'd leave that to a specialist, someone with extensive training and experience. Besides, how many of us have the time, interest, or knowledge to manage our own money—and do it well? Of all the women I've interviewed, the ones with the highest net worth didn't necessarily earn (or inherit) the most money. The whopping majority worked with financial professionals.

Caution 1: Financial professionals make lousy Prince Charmings. Don't ever hand over your money, close your eyes, turn your back, and hope they'll take good care of you. You need to be educated and involved. A good advisor will make sure you are.

How do you find a trustworthy financial professional? Ask for referrals from people who are happy with their advisors. Or go online to find names of advisors near you. Try these sites:

- www.napfa.org, the website for the National Association of Personal Financial Advisors
- www.garrettplanningnetwork.com, the Garrett Planning Network of fee-only financial advisors
- www.cfp.net, the website of Certified Financial Planner Board of Standards

Caution 2: Resist the urge to sign up with the first advisor you meet. Interview at least three. Ask questions such as these, then go with your gut:

1. Would you tell me about yourself?
2. Do you specialize in certain investments?
3. Can you describe the ideal client you like to work with?
4. How do you charge for your services, and what costs might I incur working with you?
5. How often do you communicate with clients; how often will I hear from you?
6. Have you ever been involved in any lawsuits, arbitration, or disciplinary problems?
7. Is there anything you want me to know about you that I haven't asked?

Need more help? I've written a booklet filled with great advice, *Finding a Financial Advisor You Can Trust*, available on my website (www.barbarastanny.com). I've included everything you need to know about hiring the right professional for you and making sure you protect yourself by being a good client.

Three-Step Formula for Financial Success

"Wealth is largely a result of habit."

—John Jacob Astor

We've covered a large amount of information in a very short time. You won't learn it all in one reading. And we pretty much just stuck with the basics!

I recommend my retreat participants practice the Discipline of Affluence by following this three-step formula for at least four months. You'll be amazed at what will happen. (I started doing this ages ago, and I continue to this day.)

1. Every day, read something about money. I call this the Osmosis School of Learning. Do this even if it's only a minute or two perusing the headlines of the business section or flipping through *Money* magazine, instead of *People*, while waiting in the checkout line at the market, or skimming a paragraph in a financial book before going to bed. So much of getting smart or smarter about money is a matter of familiarizing yourself with the jargon and current trends. Warning: Focus on the facts, not the hype. The media feeds on fear. Bad news sells. Do your best to ignore the drama, and just stick to educating yourself.

There are countless educational sites on the internet. My favorite are Dailyworth.com, Investopedia.com, Marketwatch.com, and The Motley Fool (fool.com/how-to-invest).

2. Every week, talk about money, especially with someone who knows more than you. Women rarely engage in financial discussions other than to moan and groan about money. When was the last time you sat down with friends or colleagues and asked how they learned about finances, how they've invested their portfolio, or for whatever advice they have?

I suggest forming a financial study group or financial book club with friends. Also check out the money clubs at Wife.org.

3. Every month, save automatically. Simply fill out a form (easy to do online) and your bank will automatically transfer money from your checking account or paycheck into a savings account. You don't miss what you don't see. Automate your investing, too, with what's known as dollar cost averaging. This means regularly transferring a certain amount of money into a mutual fund. Many of you may be thinking, "But I have nothing left over at the end of the month." If that's the case, start putting all your spare change into a jar at the end of each day. Or track your spending to see where you can make cuts. Add those savings to the jar, which you then deposit directly into your savings account every month. You'll be surprised how quickly small sums add up.

Mint.com can be very helpful because it tracks all your bank, credit, and investment accounts in one place. Bankrate.com has a terrific collection of calculators to help with planning, budgeting, and saving goals.

There's always more to learn, of course. But this is a good beginning. Understanding these basics is like knowing how to dog-paddle. You're ready to jump in and stay afloat. You might feel a little tentative at first. But the more time you spend in financial waters, the better you'll become. And the more you'll enjoy splashing around with your *Inner Financier.* Before you know it, you'll be ready to play in the deep end, the fourth and final stage of *Sacred Success.*

CHAPTER SUMMARY: Disciplined Action, Part 2—The Discipline of Affluence

- To go from being a Consumer to a Wealth Builder, you need to invest wisely.

- There are only five places to invest: stocks, bonds, real estate, cash, and commodities.

- There are only two ways to invest: own or loan.

- So many women shy away from investing, afraid of the risk. Yet our biggest risk is that we will outlive our money.

- Put at least some money in assets that grow faster than inflation and taxes.

- Sure, the markets will go up and down, but volatility only matters when you sell.

- The truth is, risk offers opportunity for gain as it does potential for loss.

- You can minimize risk through time and diversification.

- Mutual funds are a good way to diversify.

- Invest by going *up* the Investment Pyramid.

- Work with financial professionals you trust.

- Follow the three-step formula: Every day, read about money. Every week, talk about money. Every month, automatically save.

DISCIPLINE OF AFFLUENCE HOMEWORK

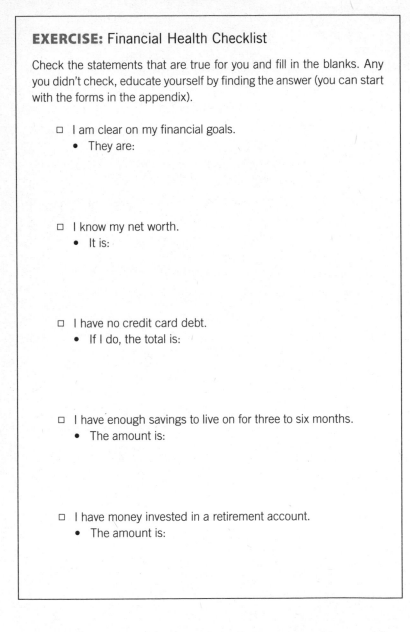

EXERCISE: Financial Health Checklist

Check the statements that are true for you and fill in the blanks. Any you didn't check, educate yourself by finding the answer (you can start with the forms in the appendix).

☐ I am clear on my financial goals.
- They are:

☐ I know my net worth.
- It is:

☐ I have no credit card debt.
- If I do, the total is:

☐ I have enough savings to live on for three to six months.
- The amount is:

☐ I have money invested in a retirement account.
- The amount is:

□ I have investments outside a retirement account.
   • The amount is:

□ I understand the investments I own.
□ I will have enough money to support myself in retirement.
□ I have a will, power of attorney, and health directive.
□ I feel assured that if I died today, my affairs would be properly handled.
□ I know where all my financial documents and records are.

CHAPTER 7

Modeling
Greatness—Stage 4

"God's voice asks one question only:
are you ready yet to help Me save the world?"

—*A Course in Miracles*

Be Mindful of What You Model

"That some should be rich shows that others may
become rich and, hence, is just encouragement to
industry and enterprise."

—*Abraham Lincoln*

I'll never forget how, shortly after I moved to California with my young daughters and gambling husband, I saw a poster that made a lasting impression. On it was written: *Will it matter that I was?* I recognized, in that instant, despite the fact my life was falling apart, that I *was* on earth for a reason.

My children were my motivation. Like a mama tiger smelling danger for her cubs, I was fiercely determined to set a better example for my girls than what they were seeing. No matter what it took, I *was* going to get smart about money! My children *mattered*. And I longed to be a better role model. Sure, I desired financial security for me and my family. But far more, I wanted to be someone my girls respected and wanted to emulate.

In the years that followed, as I confronted my fears and healed my insecurities, I could eventually say, and genuinely mean, that, yes, *I matter*. Me! I *really* do. In fact, we *all* do. That simple but profound realization became a harbinger of my highest purpose. I was determined to do whatever I could to prevent not just my kids, but all women from suffering the financial indignities I had.

Looking back, that poster was my first introduction to what I'd later identify as Stage 4, Modeling Greatness, or in the words of Mahatma Gandhi, being the change I wanted to see in the world. You model Greatness by making a difference, recognizing that you possess the power to effect change—in your family, your workplace, your community, as well as in yourself. And whenever you demonstrate Greatness—doing what you can to reduce the "world's great hunger"—you encourage others to do the same.

The truth is, we are always modeling either mediocrity or Greatness. For much of my adult life, I was the poster child for mediocrity—my choices were constrained by fear, my life hemmed in by my perceived helplessness, my Ego had free rein to run the show. Every time you and I submit to our Ego's pitiful need for safety and conformity, we're modeling mediocrity.

In contrast, we model Greatness whenever we stand by our Soul's deepest truths—even though stepping into our Greatness means stepping out of our comfort zone. This final stage is the ultimate reason we undertook this process in the first place. Here is where we fully employ our power. Here is where we enjoy enormous gratification. Here is where we not only help (and inspire) others, but imbue our own life with meaning and purpose.

However, as I've come to see, we can never truly help another heal until we first heal ourselves. Otherwise, we become what the *Course* calls *"unhealed healers,"* rendering us ineffective at best, or actually harmful. In *Sacred Success*, personal healing *is* the pathway to power. Our wounds are, in fact, the portal through which healing light may enter us, light we can ultimately share with others to illuminate their worlds and heal their wounds.

The work we've done in the three previous stages has prepared us to courageously shine our light brightly, wherever there's darkness, as healed healers and models of Greatness. The previous chapter in particular, the Discipline of Affluence, permits us to model Greatness without financial diversion.

"You can't be the light of the world," observed the Reverend Michael Beckwith, "if you can't pay your light bill!"

Meet the Women of Influence

> *"We measure abundance not by what flows in, but what flows out."*
>
> *—Brother David Steindl-Rast*

I once heard it explained that when you have more money than you need, *that's wealth*. When you use your money to make a difference, *that's power*. *Sacred Success*—which is about achieving both wealth and power—culminates in this fourth and final stage.

I believe financial success allows us, as women, to model Greatness in the grandest way. And I am genuinely heartened by where we're heading. According to the 2013 Allianz study *Women, Money, and Power*, ever since the 2008 financial crisis, there's been a major shift occurring in women's relationship with money.

As a result of that crisis, the study reported, a new demographic is emerging on the scene: *Women of Influence*. These women are not necessarily high earners, or even gainfully employed, though many are. What sets a Woman of Influence apart is that she's financially knowledgeable, "more likely to feel confident in her ability to spend, save, and invest wisely than the average woman," explains Allianz.

Granted, the survey found that only one in five women fits this profile. But as more women join their ranks by taking the financial reins, these Women of Influence are becoming global game-changers, Models of Greatness.

I see it as inevitable. Once a woman becomes financially secure, her motivation shifts from making more money to making her mark. She starts looking for opportunities to gain more influence and give back to others in ways that fill her with meaning and pleasure, while at the same time imbuing her with power and the ability to make an impact.

"When I got financially secure, I wanted to go from success to significance, to do philanthropy," a successful entrepreneur told me. Then, quoting Thornton Wilder, she added, "Money, like manure, is not worth a thing unless it's spread around."

"I have never done anything in my whole life, not one thing, for money," said another mega-earner. "I have only done what I'm passionate about because it's given me the opportunity to become more fully who I am and make a difference in the lives of others. That's where I get my joy and fulfillment."

As I mentioned in earlier chapters, if there was one theme that reverberated throughout my interviews with elite earners, it was how their inclination to help others ignited their drive to succeed, not the other way around. I constantly heard comments like these:

"I like being a role model," one woman said proudly. "People look at me and say, 'If she can have all this, why can't I have it too?'"

"It's more than money," said another about her thirty years of success. "It's impact. I am motivated by leaving a legacy."

When I asked what drove an executive who runs a multimillion-dollar division of a major corporation, she replied simply: "I want to help everyone who works for me achieve their maximum potential." Another attributed the stellar growth of her real estate firm to this fact: "I am maternal. I am a nurturer. I really try to nurture my staff. I get to help show them different ways to grow their business."

These Women of Influence offer our greatest hope for healing the planet. I believe, because you're reading this book, you are meant to be one of them—if you aren't already. As a Woman of Influence, you are in the best possible position to model Greatness. While the preceding stages were comprised of four steps, Stage 4 has only two.

Step 1: Ask Yourself: What Is the Legacy I Want to Leave?

"If you think you're too small to have an impact, try going to bed with a mosquito."

—Anita Roddick

What will your legacy be? This question cuts right to the core of why you're here and the mark you wish to leave behind after you're gone. Your desired legacy serves as an internal compass, guiding your daily decisions in the direction of your optimal future.

Every one of us leaves a legacy, but in my experience, surprisingly few reflect on what they want theirs to be. Yet it's an important point for us all to ponder. If you haven't already, now is the time to think about your legacy, and here's how to begin. Ask yourself, What do I want my obituary to say?

You've heard of Alfred Nobel, who created the Nobel Peace Prize, right? But did you know he was the inventor of dynamite and made his fortune manufacturing cannons and other weapons of destruction? In 1888 when his brother died, newspapers published Alfred's obituary by mistake. He was horrified by what he read. "The merchant of death is dead," one obituary stated. "Dr. Alfred Nobel, who became rich by finding ways to kill more people faster than ever before, died yesterday." Not wanting "death merchant" to be his lasting legacy, he bequeathed almost his entire estate to establish the Nobel Prize.

"By asking ourselves how we want to be remembered," explain authors James Kouzes and Barry Posner in their book *A Leader's Legacy*, "we plant the seeds for living our lives as if we matter." When you live your life as if *you* matter, you can't help but model Greatness.

I recently stumbled on a poignant blog written by a hospice physician. Dr. Karen Wyatt witnessed how many of her patients were "deeply disturbed" because they hadn't "contributed anything significant to life," she wrote. "The message I have taken away from these patients is that it is far better to contemplate the meaning of life when we actually have some time left to work on the question."

Your legacy need not light up the sky. It need leave only the slightest footprint in the sand. Whether you engage in a small act of kindness or a groundbreaking global initiative, you are touching lives, making a difference. The size or scope of your impact is irrelevant. As philosopher Ralph Waldo Emerson put it, "To know even one life has breathed easier because you have lived, this is to have succeeded."

All that matters is that your legacy reflects your purpose, makes you proud, brings you pleasure, and inspires or improves something or someone else.

"Every day I think about my legacy, my impact on others, especially women I work with," said Victoria Edwards, who choked up with tears telling me her story. Victoria was the advertising executive we met back in Chapter 5, who finally spoke up to the boss who'd constantly yelled at her.

"When I was at my last job, getting screamed at by my boss, I finally screamed back—knowing I was doing it for the four young girls sitting there. I purposely stood up for myself to provide a positive role model, to show that they should stand up for themselves and not be bullied by bosses. My goal was not to do it *for* them or *protect* them but to show them *a model to emulate*."

Those four young women will probably never forget that scene in their office, when Victoria met her boss head-on. That's legacy. That's leaving an imprint that inspires others. Some of you already know what you want your legacy to be. But many of you may be scratching your heads, wondering, "What's mine?"

Here's a very powerful exercise to help you get clarity:

EXERCISE: My Legacy

Close your eyes, take several deep breaths, and relax. When you're ready, imagine that you are on your deathbed, at the end of a long and meaningful life. As you lie there, ask yourself: *What gives me the most satisfaction knowing that this is what I'll be remembered for?*

Once you get a sense of what that might be, come back to this moment and write down what came to you in the space below.

Then ask yourself: What can I begin doing right now that will contribute to the legacy I wish to leave? Make a few notes here.

For insurance executive Erin, this exercise was an eye-opener. "It made me think about my significance in the world," she said. "That wasn't something I thought much about before. It allowed me to design my life with a much bigger vision and much greater impact. It's not just about me. It's how can I serve in a bigger way."

But first, she admitted, "I had to figure out how to be passionate about what I was doing." Erin, who was twenty-eight years old at the time, intentionally began designing her life in alignment with her purpose, which was to "help women support, uplift, and encourage each other to live a life they love."

She kept her day job, but redefined and expanded it. In the three years since her first retreat, under the umbrella of her agency, she has increased her marketing toward women; formed a monthly business-women's luncheon group; launched a teen mentorship program, *Gals Lead*; and is creating a similar program for women, *Living Your Life Purpose*.

"Without a doubt, this is my Soul's work," Erin told me proudly, realizing, "living my purpose, it inspires others to live theirs—just by being who I am."

I must share an email that came while I was writing this chapter; it's from successful life coach and philanthropist Victoria Trabosh. Victoria told me she'd recently had a serious heart attack.

"I could have easily died," she wrote, explaining that the unexpected scare pushed her to ponder her passing in a new way. "Honestly, I want my legacy to be that I was a great mother, grandmother, and wife. Funny isn't it? I've helped raised almost $1 million for *Itafari* [her foundation supporting Rwanda]. I have an incredible work life. Yet it all turns out to be about family. If my life today can affect those people, then my legacy will be established."

Something else she happened to mention: Since her heart attack, she said, "I'm working less and making more money."

She learned the tough way what six- and seven-figure women have consistently shown to be true. At some point, it's not the number of hours you work but your level of focus that leads to stellar success.

Step 2: Give *Powerfully.*

> *"If we treat people as they are, we make them worse.*
> *If we treat people as they ought to be, we help them*
> *become what they are capable of becoming."*
>
> —Johann Wolfgang von Goethe

There is a story of a man who walked past a beggar and asked, "Why, God, do you not do something for these people?" God replied, "I did do something. I made you."

In the end, Greatness doesn't come from what you have, but from what you *give.*

You're probably thinking, "Hey wait, I'm *already* giving plenty." No doubt that's true. As a woman, you've likely spent your entire life giving to others—your children, your neighbors, your friends, heck, even perfect strangers. Remember, the Fourth Rule of Money is Give Generously.

But there are two kinds of giving, with a world of difference between the two. One empowers. The other weakens. The latter lies in the realm of Ego, which gives with ulterior motives: to gain control, get love, impress others, foster dependency, or fix someone else.

Giving Powerfully is rooted in the Soul, whose only goal is your personal growth. Ultimately, your legacy is decided by how you share your resources—money, time, talent—to help those in need, without expectation of return and without exhausting yourself.

There are Four Rules for Giving Powerfully. They are:

1. Give to yourself first.
2. Take responsibility for yourself, and only yourself.

3. Leverage your financial clout.

4. Obey the Law of Focused Giving.

RULE 1: GIVE TO YOURSELF FIRST.

> *"Respect yourself and others will respect you."*
>
> —Confucius

Sacred Success relies heavily on your ability to receive, as we discussed in Stage 2. We all know that giving is vastly easier, infinitely more comfortable, and feels far nobler than receiving. Yet, you can never give what you have not received.

"*To give and receive are one in truth,*" the *Course* repeatedly reminds us. "*To give a thing requires first you have it in your own possession.*"

Any attempt to give more than you have always backfires. "To give until it hurts" was once a woman's implicit duty. Society rewarded sacrificing oneself to help another. And selfless giving offers the illusion of feeling needed, important, powerful. But, as many of us have learned, trying to give to others without filling ourselves up first is, in the end, an abdication of power. You'll wind up feeling depleted, resentful, depressed.

For many of the women I interviewed, this awareness was life altering. "What drove me was inadequacy, feeling like I'm not worth anything, so I always had to achieve more and give more," said a high-tech entrepreneur. "Without intentionally improving myself, it was real easy to be like a little boat in a storm, always knocked back and forth."

After a difficult few years of setbacks, then an extended period devoted to Surrender and self-improvement, she finally realized, "My primary business in my life is taking care of me."

That statement may, on the surface, sound appallingly selfish. But I saw it as quite admirable and wise. As we know by now, you can never fully help another until you first take care of yourself. Even if you have kids, parents, or a garden depending on you, you must put your oxygen mask on first to be in any condition to take care of them. Greatness must give to self first in order to support all.

Civil rights activist and poet Audre Lorde once said: "I have come to believe that caring for myself is not self-indulgent. Caring for myself is an act of survival."

To which I would add, caring for myself is an act of self-respect, the motivation for achieving financial success, and essential to living a quality life. Self-respect reflects a desire to be the best I can be, to live authentically, and to treat myself and others lovingly.

Eventually, the women in my retreats come to realize, as this one did, "It's not only okay, it's a requirement to respect myself and my needs."

The most successful women I've interviewed expressed variations on a Native American adage, "A hungry person has no charity. Always nurture yourself."

"I needed to grow myself personally as a woman, not just as a businessperson," said an entrepreneur earning millions. "I needed to pamper me, take care of me. If you can't be good to yourself, you can't be good to your employees, and they'll leave you and go somewhere else."

I was so impressed when a woman I'll call Ginny described walking away from a million-dollar salary to stay home with her child. "I value my time and my happiness," she said. "I have my priorities straight. I know I can always make money."

In *Sacred Success*, giving starts by giving to yourself first, with love, *not* guilt. Self-care, a clear sign of self-respect, becomes your number one priority. Putting yourself first may seem self-centered, but as George Sand once wrote: "Nothing resembles selfishness more closely than self-respect."

In reality, self-denial usually leads to antipathy, anger, pain, even illness—certainly not the traits you want to model or the legacy you wish to leave. Tatiana, the strategic planner and meeting facilitator mentioned earlier, articulated this so well when she told me, "I now understand the difference between taking care of myself because I'm finally *resentful* enough to do it, and taking care of myself because it is *essential*. Self-care creates flow and leads to success."

When you put yourself first, you have more vitality to model Greatness. "My selfish self-care vacation was just what my heart and soul needed," photographer Jill Martin explained in an email. "When I put myself first, I can more effortlessly give to others."

While self-care is mandatory, it's not in most women's vocabulary. Therefore, discipline is essential to keep us eating well, exercising regularly, managing our money prudently. Charlene, the Canadian executive, recognized: "It is easy to slip back into negative Nelly when I'm tired and spent. I also become needy, clingy, and insecure." This is neither the way she wants to live, nor the legacy she wishes to leave.

Self-care also requires Surrender—regularly taking time out for play, pampering, and solitude. I loved this email I got from a sales manager I'll call Celeste. "Finally after some time of stillness the voice within said, 'I declare this National Take Care of Celeste Month.'"

She immediately told her husband that there would henceforth be "no laundry, no cooking, no trying to fix the unfixable for the kids," while she took the month off.

Her husband balked a bit, she said. "Then he got busy making a shopping list and off to the grocery store he went. I was scared that this might backfire and not sure that I was doing the right thing, but after two weeks of doing laundry and receiving my gratitude notes, James gave me an easy 'Yes' when I suggested a housekeeper. I'm free! I'm free! The housekeeper starts tomorrow."

RULE 2: TAKE RESPONSIBILITY FOR YOURSELF, AND ONLY YOURSELF.

"You give but to yourself."

—A Course in Miracles

If Giving Powerfully requires putting yourself first, it also requires giving up control of others. In *Sacred Success*, your sole responsibility is YOU. Despite what you'd like to think, you can't be responsible for anyone else's actions or decisions. All you can do is make requests, set boundaries, and follow up with consequences (or rewards).

You may have been brainwashed to believe otherwise. And your Ego will vehemently oppose this point. But trying to control others is a hopeless waste of energy, a surefire way to cede your power and sap your energy. Besides, trying to govern another's actions is demeaning and disrespectful, saying in effect that they're not capable of doing it for themselves.

Taking responsibility for yourself means honoring your deepest truth and genuine needs, guarding against self-depreciation, setting clear priorities and appropriate boundaries.

Financial advisor Rebecca Bar-Shain, who lives her legacy daily—"helping people feel financially confident"—had been brought up believing she needed to be responsible for everyone around her. Finally, she came to an important realization. "I need to be clear that when I try to give to others, they can take it or not," she said. "If things don't turn out as I'd hoped, I always used to feel like I failed."

As an example, she told me that recently she spent a great deal of time helping a client create a budget. The client, however, never followed through.

"Now I realize it's her choice. I gave her the tools. There are just too many things out of my control, not just markets but people's choices," Rebecca said. At long last, she understood she wasn't accountable for another's actions nor could she let those actions decide her self-worth.

Personal responsibility is a prerequisite for realizing your power and modeling Greatness. Without it, as many women discover, your desire to help others quickly disintegrates into codependence—the tendency to focus on the needs and wants of others to the exclusion of your own—a disempowering condition women have struggled with for centuries.

Greatness and codependency can't coexist. In *Sacred Success*, we are seeking to strengthen and gain control of ourselves, not others.

RULE 3: LEVERAGE YOUR FINANCIAL CLOUT.

"There are those who give with joy, and that joy is their reward."

—*Kahlil Gibran*

I remember nutrition store owner Suzy Carroll sharing an epiphany she had at the retreat. "I always felt a level of guilt around selling [nutritional] products to make money. I've often said I'd rather just give them away," she declared. "No more of that! Going forward, I will embrace the sacredness of receiving and giving by building a prosperous business so I can then help more people." Much later, she said with genuine enthusiasm, "I started the ball rolling to form a nonprofit that grants funds for holistic care, something I've thought about for years."

Philanthropy, which comes from the Greek word meaning *"the love of humanity,"* can be our most powerful tool for modeling Greatness. Many women, however, disqualify themselves as philanthropists because, if they're not a Carnegie or Rockefeller, they don't believe they have enough. Others, if they're not the breadwinners, think charitable donations are their spouse's responsibility.

Still, no matter how much money a woman has, if she's lacking confidence and/or knowledge around money, she'll be reluctant to give. The number one reason women don't donate is economic insecurity. I often hear from women in my retreats: "I wish I could give more but I've squandered so much over the years."

The good news: You don't need huge wads of cash to make a considerable difference.

Cyndy Bragg, for example, produced and hosted an "all-gal comedy festival for a ladies-only audience to inspire women, through humor, to quit playing the victim game." She gave a portion of the proceeds to a women's charitable organization. "It was thrilling to produce and host this event," she effused, "but making a donation to 'Suited for Change' actually made me feel like a much grander person. I could give while having a blast."

Yoga teacher Stephanie Slawek heard about "a creative-sounding event on Valentine's Day that was being offered at a pay-what-you-can rate. I decided to pay the full price. It felt scary and exciting and liberating to pay more than my small self thought I 'should.'"

Modeling Greatness includes even the smallest acts of generosity, which can not only affect the beneficiary but boost your own self-esteem and sense of fulfillment. However, to really leverage your financial clout, to leave an enduring legacy with maximum effect, you're better off combining your contribution with other people's. Doing so can add significantly more weight to your single donation. Collectively, women have the power to create enormous social change.

There are all sorts of vehicles to do this, including:

- *Giving Circles* (gatherings of individuals who pool their money and choose the recipient together).

- *Family Foundations* (private nonprofit organizations created and funded by a particular family).

- *Donor-Advised Funds* (an account set up by an individual but maintained and operated by a specific charity).

- *Women-Focused Groups* (such as Women Moving Millions, a nonprofit whose members pledge at least a million dollars; Global Fund for Women, the world's largest foundation dedicated to women's rights internationally; Women Donors Network, whose members pledge six-figure donations; and the Red Cross's Tiffany Circles, women who donate $10,000 to their local chapters).

Leveraged giving can be easy to overlook and sometimes compli-cated to carry out. You want to make sure you get the full tax benefits for your charitable contributions. I highly recommend seeking professional advice from a reputable estate attorney, a financial advisor, and a CPA to help you ascertain how much is possible and advantageous to give. Furthermore, nine out of ten people don't mention charities in their will. So if a professional doesn't bring it up, be sure you do.

RULE 4: OBEY THE LAW OF FOCUSED GIVING.

"The extraordinary life is waiting quietly beneath the skin of all that is ordinary."

—*Mark Nepo*

To make sure your financial giving is powerful, not pointless, profligate, or actually detrimental, you must obey the Law of Focused Giving, which states: *Giving, like light, is most powerful when it's most focused.* Spontaneously dropping small change into plastic jars for charity on supermarket counters may be a lovely gesture, but it's not necessarily the optimal use of your philanthropic dollars.

Unfocused, random, or impulsive giving can result in reduced or negative effectiveness, personal resentment, and even a sense of depriva-tion and scarcity. How often do we thoughtlessly give money to others, especially our children or family members, perhaps robbing them of their self-esteem; diminishing their drive; enabling, not empowering them? How often do we blindly give more than we can afford, endanger-ing our future, causing ourselves needless suffering and sorrow? How often do we give only because we think we *should*, because we feel guilty if we don't, and end up embittered?

Focused giving is giving with boundaries. This means your chari-table contributions are based on a well-thought-out plan that reflects your values, your passion, and your purpose. *Planned giving is powerful giving.*

Philanthropy, however, is often the least thought-out, most disorganized part of our financial activities. Most of us give more attention to selecting a pair of shoes than to where we donate our dollars. But the more strategic deliberation you give to your charitable contributions, the more bang you get from your buck—financially, socially, emotionally.

The Women's Philanthropy Institute reports that "women generally donate more than men, but they give in much smaller amounts to twice as many organizations." Haphazard giving significantly dilutes your influence and often your satisfaction. Focused giving ensures you use your money for maximum traction rather than being tempted by every telephone solicitation or personal appeal that comes your way. Initially, Suzy told me, she'd give "a little bit here and there, but I was pulling it out of my savings and it felt more like a 'should.'"

After her second *Sacred Success* retreat, she said, "I went through my finances and really fine-tuned everything." When she realized she had extra money, she set up a separate account she labeled her "Donation Fund." Every month, a designated amount goes into that fund. "It's not a lot, but it's great to know I can do it without dipping into my retirement or vacation fund. My vacations are very important to me."

"Do you and your husband have to agree?" I asked her.

"When we donate bigger chunks we definitely discuss it. And I love being able to do that."

Many of the women I've interviewed made focused giving a family affair. They used philanthropy to build a stronger relationship with their partner and teach their kids about values, money management, and life goals. And yet, although 73 percent of women feel that passing money on to their children and causes that matter to them is important, only 14 percent have done anything to ensure that this will happen.

Leading by Example

> *"Each person must see himself as though the entire world were held in balance and any deed he might do could tip the scales."*
>
> —*Maimonides*

I am reminded, as I conclude this chapter, of what my dear friend and teacher extraordinaire Jill Rogers often asks in her classes for women: "If the whole world were following you, would you be happy where you're taking them?"

You may or may not see yourself as a leader. Nevertheless, you often have considerable bearing on the many people who cross your path. Everyone stands to gain when you thoughtfully reflect on the legacy you wish to leave and then give back to the world in ways that are both empowering to others and replenishing to yourself. You'll know you're modeling Greatness when you can say, with a satisfied sigh, "Yes, I'm happy with the example I'm setting for others. I'm proud of where I'm going. And I feel really good about myself."

CHAPTER SUMMARY: Modeling Greatness—Stage 4

- Modeling Greatness means making a difference by recognizing that you possess the power to effect change—in your family, your workplace, your community, as well as in yourself.

- You are always modeling, either mediocrity or Greatness.

- You can never truly help another heal until you first heal yourself, which is the work we've been doing throughout this book.

- Financial success allows you to model Greatness in the grandest way.

- A new demographic is emerging—*Women of Influence*—who knowledgeably and confidently manage their money.

- These Women of Influence are in the best possible position to model Greatness by giving generously. You are meant to be one of them, if you aren't already.

- Two Steps to Model Greatness:
  - Step 1: Ask yourself: What is the legacy I want to leave?
  - Step 2: Give *powerfully*.
    - Rule 1: Give to yourself first.
    - Rule 2: Take responsibility for yourself, and only yourself.
    - Rule 3: Leverage your financial clout.
    - Rule 4: Obey the Law of Focused Giving.

STAGE 4 HOMEWORK

EXERCISE: Leaving a Legacy Checklist

To help you ponder your legacy, ask yourself the following questions, then jot down your answers below.

1. How do I want people to remember me?

2. What changes would I like to see in the world?

3. What do I value most?

4. Does my giving reflect my values?

5. How can I use my money to pass on my wisdom and values to my children?

PART THREE

The Power

CHAPTER 8

Welcoming the Warrior

"It's not up to you what you learn, but only whether you learn through joy or through pain."

—*A Course in Miracles*

When All Hell Breaks Loose

"I live in the quiet calm of certainty."

—*A Course in Miracles*

At the conclusion of my *Sacred Success* retreats, I always issue a warning: *When you commit to Greatness, everything unlike itself will come up to be healed.* Life gets in the way. Obstacles arise. Shit happens. Breakdowns occur. This, of course, is your Ego conspiring to throw you off course. You'll need to concentrate on your Soul's wisdom to resist your Ego's cunning. Otherwise, it's easy to lose your footing, succumb to fear, become hamstrung by your own tenacious habits, or get sucked into the mainstream mentality.

To the mainstream, obstacles are like ticking time bombs, something to quickly defuse or preferably avoid altogether. But for the Soul, obstacles are doorways to healing. What seems to get *in* the way is *the* way to transformation.

As *A Course in Miracles* affirms, "*Trials are but lessons that you failed to learn presented once again, so where you made a faulty choice before you can now make a better one and thus escape all pain that what you chose before has brought you.*"

Difficulties are not diversions from Greatness but evidence of dysfunctional patterns that must be corrected in order to follow your calling. Every challenge provides the chance to respond in a new way. Your Soul is saying: "Choose again, not as you have in the past."

Reframing problems, as we've learned, is an act of receiving. By responding differently you'll invariably receive radically different, and hopefully vastly improved, results. Every ordeal—from the computer crashing to a spat with your spouse—is an opportunity to transmute your past into a better future by reacting differently than you normally would.

After a recent retreat, where she'd been exploring new business ideas, a woman I'll call Carla explained in an email how rough her first week home had been. "I had an intense, difficult discussion with my man," she wrote, "and a really unpleasant interaction with my mother."

Carla reacted with "torrents of anger, frustration, doubt, confusion that left me feeling more anxious and afraid than I have in a long time."

Her instinctive response was to slip into old patterns of self-depreciation and denial. "I had a strong and pervasive fear that what I'm doing, who I am, is not enough. And at the same time, my immediate desire was to 'do' something to escape these feelings." She knew these crippling insecurities had been her lifelong companions, but then she remembered: "Once we commit to our Greatness, everything that is out of alignment with our calling will come up to be healed. I feel that this is what's happening for me. It is powerful and I am grateful."

Instead of suppressing her emotions, Carla surrendered to them. "It actually feels like I am feeling everything I was sad about in the past few years but didn't really have the space to feel—sadness about my divorce, about the death of my grandmother, anger about the ways that some people I trusted disappointed me. Just a lot of feelings!" she said.

Allowing her emotions to surface freed her in unexpected ways. A later update was decidedly different. "I spoke to my mother directly about our frustrating conversation. I'm proud of the way I'm directly addressing the things that make me angry," she wrote. "I needed some time off, so I gave myself the gift of actually taking it. I never ever would've done this before. But I can feel my creativity starting to, very slowly, ooze back in.

"I've started to see more clearly what my business idea could be, and to actually trust that I can create it. I am building an amazing team of people around me who want to work on, and support, my business. I am setting all sorts of boundaries and having all kinds of tough conversations. And I was fully reimbursed for my work over the summer, which has been outstanding for two months. I finally found a way to ask directly but also respectfully for what I was owed."

Rather than viewing her difficult issues as irritating impediments, Carla used them to practice the alchemy of *Sacred Success*, finding the "good" in the "bad," which allowed her to see her next steps clearly. One woman described this alchemical process in an email: "I am learning to recognize doors where I thought there were only walls."

Maintaining this perspective—seeing difficulties as doors, not walls—can be tough. The force of your Ego and the ease of mediocrity exert an intense pull that's always at play. It takes the willingness to surrender and a disciplined mind not to succumb.

The Missing Link

"It is the Warrior's task to become visible and through example and intention to empower and inspire others."

—Angeles Arrien

As we approach the end of our time together, remember that *Sacred Success* is a continuing process, an ongoing practice. Whenever you're tempted to fall prey to fear and forfeit your power, the way to proceed, paraphrasing *A Course in Miracles*, is to turn inward, *seeking and finding all the barriers within yourself that you've built against your own empowerment.*

You've explored many of your internal barriers in the previous pages—something you will continue to do whenever you feel stuck, stalled, or snowed under. However, as I've learned from follow-up correspondence with *Sacred Success* graduates, there are four particularly insidious barriers that you need to be aware of lest you fall victim to them. I call these barriers Pollutants to Power because they are the Ego's toxic spill and, if ignored, will contaminate your integrity, weaken your determination, smother your passion. The four most virulent are: Perfectionism, Impatience, Isolation, and Guilt.

But before we delve into these four Pollutants, let's reflect, for a moment, on how far we've come in our Heroine's Journey. Whether you realize it or not, you have by now unearthed the treasure you've been seeking. Like Dorothy's slippers in the land of Oz, this treasure has been with you all along, though buried deep within, far from awareness. The treasure to which I refer is a deep-seated source of strength, daring, and focus, otherwise known as the Warrior Archetype, the psychological blueprint for leadership and courage, for fierce determination in the face of interminable obstacles.

I believe this archetype provides the missing link in women's evolution. The Warrior holds the hardwiring for power. The Warrior also holds the antidote to all Pollutants.

Unfortunately, a lot of women shun this archetype. They wrongly equate Warrior energy with destruction and violence. As a result, too many have atrophied Warriors that show up as passivity and cowardice, compliance or rebellion, refusing to claim personal authority or projecting their authority onto others. A woman with a stifled Warrior remains a victim, unable to passionately and tenaciously pursue her purpose.

The Warrior Archetype is neither violent nor vicious—that's the Ego's ruthless attempt to retain dominance. The Warrior is the guardian of the Soul, custodian of your power. According to the Tibetan Buddhist tradition,* *a Warrior is one who is not afraid of herself.*

Isn't that what we've been doing throughout this book—Warrior training? Learning to love and accept who we are—our light and our shadows, our achievements and our failures—rather than fear, despise, or reject any of it. As Erich Fromm told us the first chapter, "the main task in life is to give birth to our self to become what we actually are." That task is the essence of power and the crucial challenge facing women today. Our fear of *becoming who we actually are* is what produced our resistance to, and separation from, our power in the first place.

What we're apt to fear most is not our baser impulses but our most lofty ones; not our shortcomings but our strengths, our talents, our gifts of Greatness. Welcoming our Warrior allows us to fully claim, without fear or false humility, our genuine magnitude and glory.

Remember the rallying cry of *Sacred Success*, first uttered by Charlene White: "I cannot, I will not, be less than who I am for anybody."

The Four Pollutants

> *"You are more powerful than you know; you are beautiful just as you are."*
>
> —Melissa Etheridge

Keeping our Warrior in mind, let's examine the four major Pollutants to Power and the potent antidotes we have at our disposal.

---

*Thanks to Susan Piver for sharing this beautiful interpretation.

POLLUTANT 1: PERFECTIONISM.

"Believing you can be perfect is the fatal imperfection."

—*Richard Strozzi-Heckler*

Perfectionism is the archenemy of power, the kryptonite to Greatness, a noxious stance that slows us down or stops us completely. Those who are fearful of not doing it right or consistently dwell on all that could go wrong find endless excuses not to act for fear of being exposed as flawed or inadequate. Perfectionism inevitably produces paralysis.

To achieve Greatness, you must be willing to grab unexpected opportunities, plunge into the unknown, do what you're scared to do with no guarantees of success.

The Warrior's antidote to perfectionism calls for large doses of courage to stretch beyond your comfort zone and the discipline to speak a new story (even before you fully believe it).

Julie Anne was one of those perfectionists, always plagued with anxiety, convinced "I'm about to f**k up whatever I'm getting ready to do." She told me, "This angst has been so constant and pervasive, I didn't recognize the depth of it. But now that I'm seeing it, I'm practicing a new story: *'Whatever I'm about to do doesn't need to be perfect!'* What an easier, happier way to go through life!"

The Warrior's antidote also calls for a heaping measure of self-trust. I once had a teacher who defined self-trust as *knowing you can clean up what you mess up.* That simple phrase freed me forever from my own prison of perfectionism, giving me, as Charlene put it, "the freedom to be human, to make mistakes, to not be perfect and love myself no matter what happens."

Suzanne Hanger, a residential real estate agent at the time, discovered one of her clients was selling a commercial building. "In the past I would have told myself I am not qualified to sell a commercial building. I better stay away from it because I might mess it up," she told me. "But instead I heard, 'When you screw up you can clean it up.' I had no idea if I could do it or not. But I figured I would keep trying until I either got the deal or someone else did."

A few months later, Suzanne sold her client's property. "And I didn't mess anything up," she exclaimed, "because I found the secret: For everything I don't know, I know someone who knows. I can just call them—and they'll tell me what to do or better yet, they'll do it for me! I can do ANYTHING now!"

POLLUTANT 2: IMPATIENCE.

"Nature does not hurry, yet everything is accomplished."

—Lao-Tzu

At the very heart of *Sacred Success* beats a deep-seated sense of purpose. There's nothing like a stirring mission, a rousing vision, to inspire you to go for it full throttle. But when the fire in your belly rages out of control, your determination can backfire and your deep-seated purpose can be reduced to ashes. Your drive turns destructive. Your heady enthusiasm takes on an air of desperation. You are convinced that if you don't make it happen right *now*, it never will.

Impatience, like perfectionism, is fear based. Your Ego, sounding like an angry parent, is yelling, "Hurry up or you'll fall behind." These bogus threats are guaranteed to sap creativity, drain energy, and delay progress. Mediocrity is all about pushing and forcing things to happen. Greatness is all about allowing life to unfold at its own pace. Acceptance is the Warrior's antidote for unbridled impatience. Or as the *Course* simply advises: *"Let it be what it is."*

My most memorable lesson in acceptance came during an early visit to a California farm where my daughter interned. The week I was there, the seedlings in the greenhouse were sprouting and needed to be planted. The former chicks, now mature hens, had to be moved to bigger quarters. But nature had other plans. It poured. And rain was forecast for the next few days.

"You can't plant when it rains," Anna explained. "The fields are too fragile. And the ground's too wet to drive the truck to the other henhouse."

Here we were, all geared up to do both. I watched in awe at what happened next. No one got uptight. No one cursed nature. No teeth were gnashing or hands wringing. Instead, the farm owner shrugged his shoulders, and said: "Enjoy the downtime." What a concept!

We found other things to do. We cleaned the eggs. We did outreach. One woman made a delicious apple crisp. Another couple worked on a brochure. We had a scrumptious stir-fry, loaded with freshly picked veggies.

What really struck me: Everyone seemed grounded in a deep sense of faith—a respect for nature's timing, a deference to forces out of their control, a trust in a higher order—that was so strong, they were able to dispense with their plans, embrace the delays, go with the flow, and enjoy the whole process, with nary a complaint. Eventually the seeds were planted and the hens were moved, both in more than enough time.

Acceptance isn't just tolerating delays, but honoring the natural rhythm of growth. Your Ego will try to fight the current, out-control the cosmos. But your Soul wants you to kick back and "*let it be what it is*," delighting in the downtime, trusting in the outcome, even if it feels as if you're going nowhere.

POLLUTANT 3: ISOLATION.

"When you become willing to hide nothing, you will understand peace and joy."

—A Course in Miracles

As we discussed earlier, women tend be lone rangers, reluctant to ask for support, worried about imposing or deeming themselves undeserving.

Granted, seclusion plays a key role in *Sacred Success*. But only as a temporary condition of Surrender, necessary to eliminate interruption to self-contemplation.

Prolonged isolation can be a petri dish for mounting insecurity. Without feedback from others, the Ego easily takes over, permitting fear to multiply unchecked. It's easy to become fixated on our flaws, obsessed with our inadequacies, convinced we will fail or something awful will happen. In our preoccupation with self-protection, we can inadvertently push people away.

The Warrior's antidote for isolation calls for the courage to reach out and ask others to hold you accountable while you do the same for them, and the willingness to be vulnerable. There's incredible power when the empowered and enlightened gather together. Communities of like-minded women, engaged in positive change, inspire, encourage, and mentor each other, and as they do, they pay it forward, generating a ripple effect on our collective reality.

In an earlier chapter I talked about finding spotters, as men do in gyms. Spotters urge us to keep going when the going gets tough or high-five us when we finally lift that heavier weight. My spotters group has been meeting monthly for over two years. Each one of us has grown considerably.

Here's how it works: Once a month, five of us gather after work, around four thirty, at someone's house. One woman has moved out of state, so we Skype her in. The hostess serves snacks and provides tissues but no alcohol. Each person takes her turn, sharing what's on her mind, be it a troublesome situation or a thrilling victory. The others offer loving support and candid feedback, often relating their own similar experiences. Our meetings usually last about two hours. We don't leave without setting another date when we're all available. Not an easy task for busy women, but we've made it work.

I encourage *Sacred Success* graduates to form their own spotters groups with women who are on the same wavelength. Those who have done so email me with rave reviews:

"Our spotters group met last Saturday and once again, we left inspired, uplifted, supported," writes Suzy Carroll. "How wonderful to have a group of women where we can share anything and everything, our deepest emotions, moving them through to breakthroughs, crying tears and laughing like I haven't in years. How much we can learn from each other!"

"I'm so grateful for my spotters group," Natalia Volz, grief recovery specialist, told me. "They always give me a fresh perspective. They think of things that hadn't occurred to me. They remind me to live my truth, and encourage me to take exquisite care of myself."

"I'm seeing my value through my spotters group," says Charlene. "It's been a great learning experience for me, to see my value in just being who I am versus working my ass off to prove myself."

Another *Sacred Success* participant, Christine Hook, wrote this: "With the help of my spotters group, I see how I've been blowing things out of proportion, slowing myself down, and feeding my fears around my upcoming workshop."

If you do only one thing after reading this book, the most valuable would be forming your own spotters group. This single step, alone, could be your ticket to Greatness.

POLLUTANT 4: GUILT.

> *"Whenever you respond to your ego, you will experience guilt, and you will fear punishment."*
>
> —A Course in Miracles

There's an old joke: *What do you call a woman who feels no guilt? A man.* It may be funny. But sadly it's true. In fact, a recent study confirmed that women suffer significantly more guilt than men.

Guilt, simply put, is feeling as if you've done something wrong or bad. When you first add *Sacred Success* to your life, your levels of guilt will likely shoot off the charts. Every time your Soul asks you to deviate from the norm, leave your comfort zone, your Ego goes berserk, using guilt like a whip to keep you in check, warning of dreadful consequences if you disobey its rules.

It's challenging, at best, to do something like, say, spend a few days, or even a few hours, sitting on the sofa, staring out the window, without feeling like a loser or slacker. And putting yourself first, saying no to another who needs you? Gasp! People will think you're a terrible person; the guilt will become intolerable. You won't want anything to do with *Sacred Success*, at least not for very long. Yet going against the grain is exactly what Greatness requires.

As a very wise person once explained to me, "Guilt is anger you don't feel you have a right to have." Guilt is self-destructive, immobilizing, a shortcut to mediocrity, and a hindrance to healing. You know you're acting from guilt when you hear yourself saying *I should* . . . As our wonderful songstress, Athena Burke, tells women in the retreat, "Anything that comes after *I should* . . . is a lie." Our Ego's lie.

The Warrior's antidote to guilt calls for mustering up the mental discipline to STOP—stop judging, stop self-flagellating, stop panicking. Then turn to your spotters group, your love nest, or your BFF for reassurance and support in trusting your truth and honoring your needs (even if it looks to the world like you're being lazy or selfish).

Remember Tracey, the former TV producer who first glimpsed her suppressed rage as she hit the wall with a towel? When I last talked to her, she joyously told me, "I'm emerging from a cocoon into a new life." She had taken a "bridge job" as a dog walker to generate steady income giving her time to patiently figure out her next career move.

"I feel happy to the core," she declared. And I could tell she truly meant it. "Last year I was craving quiet time. I look back and remember how guilty I felt doing nothing but sitting on the couch and feeling my feelings. But I made myself do it. And I'm so grateful that I did!"

The Principal Pollutant

"The mind asks, 'Where can I go for protection?' to
which the ego replies, 'Turn to me.'"

—*A Course in Miracles*

There are other Pollutants, of course, such as repressed emotions or unresolved issues. But every one of them shares a common denominator: your Ego trying to destabilize you with its devilish ploys. You may be tempted—because it feels so normal—to take the Ego's tirades as truth. You've been doing just that since childhood. Your Ego taught you self-preservation. It felt like your friend back then. But now it's unquestionably your foe. Never forget: What saved you as a child will suffocate you as an adult.

Rather than capitulating to the Ego's false alarms or engaging in its senseless arguments, the Warrior understands that when the Ego tries to undermine you, it's actually (in its own twisted way) seeking to protect you. When your Warrior's intact, you can deliberately shift your attention from the Ego to the Soul, from fear to love, from frenzy to faith.

Luci, the musician, found it helpful to make a list of her Ego's typical phrases. Her Ego voice, she realized, said things like:

- You're not doing it right.
- You SHOULD do that, you SHOULDN'T do this.
- You ought to be doing what everyone else is doing.
- Hurry up.
- You're too old.
- There's not enough time.
- There's not enough money/creativity/energy, etc.
- They do it better and you'll never be that good (or any negative comparatives).

"I have learned that anything along these lines is the Ego voice," Luci told me. "I thank him for his concern for me, for wanting me to live the best life I possibly can. And suddenly he's quieter. Then I ask the Soul voice what she thinks. She's always so concise. She grounds me."

Going Forward

> *"No one can teach the path. One must walk the path."*
>
> —*Zen proverb*

We wrap up this chapter with gratitude for the treasure you've found in the course of reading this book, your Warrior Archetype. When you courageously and compassionately accept *all* of who you are and what you're here to do, you tap into a wellspring of astonishing strength, allowing yourself to acknowledge your Ego without acquiescing to it while staying firmly grounded in your Soul. You can rely on your Warrior's reinforcement, no longer requiring your Ego's protection. You become focused, audacious, fervently driven by a noble vision. Your truth becomes your sword. Your transparency serves as your shield.

By embracing your Warrior, you're embodying your power. The more you can rely on the Warrior within, the easier it will become to stay on the path of *Sacred Success*. And somewhere along the way, don't be surprised if, one day, you wake up and suddenly realize you are capable of moving mountains. What's more, you always have been.

CHAPTER SUMMARY: Welcoming the Warrior

- When you commit to Greatness, everything unlike itself will come up to be healed; obstacles inevitably arise.

- To the Ego, obstacles get in the way of progress. But for the Soul, obstacles are *the* doorways to healing.

- Every challenge is your Soul urging you to respond differently, not as you have in the past.

- The four most virulent Pollutants of Power are perfectionism, impatience, isolation, and guilt.

- The Warrior Archetype holds the hardwiring for power and the antidote to all Pollutants.

- The Warrior Archetype is neither violent nor vicious, but, according to the Tibetan Buddhist tradition, a Warrior *is one who is not afraid of herself.*

- Fear of becoming who you actually are is what produced your resistance to, and separation from, your power in the first place.

- Your Warrior allows you to fully claim your magnitude and glory.

- The Principal Pollutant is the Ego, which, in its twisted way, is trying to protect you. But with your Warrior intact, you no longer need your Ego's protection.

- The more you can rely on the Warrior within, the easier it will become to stay on the path of *Sacred Success.*

CREATING A SPOTTERS GROUP: SUZY CARROLL'S ELEVEN POWERFUL POINTERS*

I have enjoyed many life-enhancing, powerful experiences, but forming a spotters group, the opportunity to clean out those internal dust bunnies that collect every single month, has hands down been the most powerful and supportive experience I am blessed to have in my life every single month.

Inspired? Here are a few pointers to forming your own spotters group.

1. Interview each potential spotter sister beforehand. Are they on a similar path? Are they willing to commit to a meeting monthly? Are they comfortable with the other women you have asked? Will they honor the sacred privacy of what is shared?

2. No alcohol! This isn't a party, ladies! You are at the gym of self-growth! Alcohol causes the heavier weight to wobble. This is about clarity and truth—unimpaired.

3. We meet at 4:30 P.M. and usually wrap up by 7:00, but have been known to meet past 8:00. Heads up to your family at home! We finish when we are done, not by the clock.

4. Begin the meeting by calling in sacred space. We begin our gatherings in a way that speaks to us (discover what speaks to you). A candle is lit and we begin.

5. Someone always says, "Who wants to go first?" We go with the flow.

6. We share until we are done. Then simply say, "I'm complete." Spotter sisters will offer ideas, thoughts, and different perspectives. But mostly, we allow the person sharing to go as deep as she desires without interruption. Let your intuition be the lead.

---

*This was taken, with permission, from a newsletter written by retreat graduate Suzy Carroll.

7. While sharing, if the person pauses, let her be with her silence. We women are so quick to jump to "fix it" mode. As Barbara says, there is value in the void. What a joy to be in a space that is so safe, we can pause and let our thoughts form and our tears flow, instead of feeling pushed to keep speaking.

8. Don't worry if you arrive thinking you have nothing to say. While listening something always comes up. And if not, that is fine too.

9. If possible, have a set day and time each month. And always schedule your next meeting before heading home for the evening.

10. Be prepared to go deeper and become closer to yourself and your spotter sisters than ever imagined.

11. Have a box of Kleenex close by.

CHAPTER 9

Women Waking;
Mountains Moving

"There is no journey, only an awakening."

—*A Course in Miracles*

Something Is Happening

"When sleeping women wake, mountains move."

—*Chinese proverb*

On September 21, 2011, President Barack Obama declared in a speech to the United Nations, "Something is happening in our world. The way things have been is not the way they will be."

One thing that is happening: We've reached a tipping point in women's relationship with power. Sleeping women are waking up; embracing their power, personally and economically; infusing feminine principles into our patriarchally lopsided planet, triggering a paradigm shift of major proportions.

"We're on the brink of a massive power shift, a grinding of the gears of history into a new human condition," Maddy Dychtwald declares in her book *Influence*. "It's a world where women can, if they choose, seize the reins of economic control."

Indeed, as more women seize financial control of their own lives, they are challenging the prevailing system. Refusing to pursue the top-down male model of control, domination, and self-aggrandizement, women are adhering to distinctly female qualities rooted in collaboration, nurturing, and relationship building. This is what executive coach Linda Lawless describes as the Mutual Empowerment Model—"Enhancing the power of other people while simultaneously increasing their own power."

Unwilling to play by the old rules, women are writing new ones. Clelia Peters, a poised and statuesque thirtysomething who attended my retreat, is a perfect example. After earning her MBA, she joined a prestigious consulting firm, BCG. Extremely intelligent and highly ambitious, she never made less than $150,000 a year.

"I felt very supported at BCG. There was no glass ceiling," Clelia told me. "I like being successful. I wanted to succeed. But when I saw how many of those who were succeeding were living and working, I wanted out. Work dominated their lives to the exclusion of everything else. Many of the people who were the most successful seemed driven by fear. They weren't the smartest, or most talented, but had the most endurance. They could stomach the demands of the job, and all the stress. But it took a huge toll on me, physically and psychologically. I was always frightened, amped up, and hyperaware."

Now, between jobs doing consulting on her own, Clelia sees herself, along with countless other women, as "canaries in the coal mine" because, she explained, "we have much less tolerance for an Ego-based system." Yet, in the next breath, she added enthusiastically, "I consider this the most exciting time to be a woman in the last twenty-five hundred years."

She's not alone in this sentiment. A recent article on Bloomberg .com declared, "Women's empowerment looks to be one of the transformative economic trends of the 21st century."

The world is sitting up and taking note. The traits most associated with the feminine are increasingly being valued by and incorporated into the predominantly male culture, with compelling results. As the

Wall Street Journal reported in 2011, "Profits at Fortune 500 firms that most aggressively promoted women have been shown to be 34 percent higher than industry medians." Other studies point to similar profit surges in companies with more women on corporate boards.

"The kinds of companies we admire today are also those that depend increasingly on female attributes," *Fast Company* magazine wrote in December 2007.

This shift is occurring not only in the workplace, but in families, at PTA meetings, wherever people gather together. The so-called *women effect* is transforming the historical norm into what's becoming a clearly and increasingly preferred leadership style.

"Today that kind of command-and-control leadership has given way to a new approach," says Harvard professor and former advisor to four presidents David Gergen in his introduction to *Enlightened Power: How Women Are Transforming the Practice of Leadership.* "When we describe the new leadership, we employ terms like *consensual, relational, web-based, caring, inclusive, open, transparent*—all qualities that we associate with the 'feminine' style of leadership."

Make no mistake. This is not men versus women. We each have strengths to bring to the party. What's needed is a synthesis and celebration of both genders. As the feminine energy—which resides in both sexes (though it's often repressed in men)—is equally valued alongside the masculine, partnership will replace polarization.

Or as biological anthropologist Helen Fisher so eloquently put it, "Men and women are like two feet; they can help each other get ahead."

This is what's starting to happen. While the patriarchy slowly crumbles because it no longer works, the culture is taking what writer Sam Keen calls "a journey beyond gender," evolving into a partnership society. We no longer need fear being fully ourselves, in all our femininity, wielding our clout on our own terms. Finally, it's fun to be a woman.

Navigating the New Paradigm

*"The difficulty lies not so much in developing new
ideas as in escaping from old ones."*

—*John Maynard Keynes*

For us, as women, to adapt to this new narrative and consistently conduct ourselves with authenticity, transparency, and integrity (all hallmarks of the new paradigm)—and do so in a world that has patently revered and rewarded masculine principles—requires a dramatic shift in the way we've historically been thinking, acting, and perceiving the world.

Sacred Success is the transformational process we need for navigating the new paradigm, blending the feminine qualities of receiving and reflecting, cooperation and caring, with the masculine qualities of action and strategizing, assertiveness and toughening up. As we hone the strengths of both sexes within ourselves, merging them into an internal energetic balance, we'll become a catalytic force, or in the words of the *Course,* "*a power surge that can literally move mountains.*"

The four stages of *Sacred Success* provide the essential instructions for traveling this new terrain. All that's required is that you recognize which stage you're in and take the required steps, discussed at length in the previous five chapters.

Stage 1, the Call to Greatness, begins with a signal from your Soul, often in the form of discomfort, urging you to "stop what you're doing. Pay attention. You are being summoned to a higher level. You're ready to play a bigger game."

With the Call comes a choice. In the old paradigm, you either ignored the Call completely or valiantly forged ahead, fueled by fear, holding fast to the familiar. Instead of stopping to surrender, you made a beeline to busyness. You chose struggle and exertion over Disciplined Action. In a very short time, you'd joined the masses who model mediocrity.

In *Sacred Success*, you choose to enter **Stage 2, Receptive Surrender**, giving up control and taking time out for personal healing, for hearing your Soul's wisdom, for clarifying your highest purpose. At some point, you'll slip into **Stage 3, Disciplined Action**, stretching boldly beyond what feels secure to what seems scary in order to pursue your purpose, exercise your power, and go for Greatness with everything you've got.

When the Call comes again, as it always does, you once more step back into Receptive Surrender, maybe for just a moment or maybe longer, to reflect and regroup until you're ready to burst forth into Disciplined Action with renewed clarity and vigor. This to-and-fro dance of the stages brings you ever closer to **the final stage, where true power lies—Modeling Greatness**—by leaving a legacy, using your resources to make a difference.

Sacred Success delivers one overarching message: Yes, there *is* another way, a better way, and the four stages will lead you directly to it.

On the last morning of my four-day retreat, I lead a guided meditation. I invite you to try it now. Read the exercise below, and either record the words or memorize the questions to ask. Then go into meditation. When you're done, jot down any discoveries in the space below.

EXERCISE: Meeting My Powerful Self

This exercise is a silent meditation. Find a comfortable position, close your eyes, and imagine a golden light of relaxation flowing through your body, from your head to your neck and arms, through your chest, back, and buttocks, down your legs and feet.

When you're fully relaxed, visualize a figure standing next to you. This figure is you in the future, say, five years from now. This is your Powerful Self, an even more empowered version of you. Greet her and let her know you have some questions for her.

Ask her:

- What has been most helpful since she read this book?
- How does she spend her day?
- What's the legacy she wants you to leave?
- Is there anything more you need to know about your purpose?
- Where do you need to pay closer attention to the murmurings of your Soul?
- Is there any other advice she wishes to give you or anything she wants you to know?

Don't force anything. Let her speak. If you can't specifically "see" or "hear" her, pay attention to what comes up for you, how you feel. Be patient. The answers may not surface in this sitting, but instead later, in the weeks to come. Keep in mind, your Powerful Self is there for you anytime you need her.

What did you discover?

The Journey Continues

> *"Women, if the soul of the nation is to be saved, I believe you must become its soul."*
>
> —*Coretta Scott King*

Together we have taken a Rite of Passage into your power, preparing you to play an important role in the emerging paradigm. What that role is, you may not yet know. But know this: The changes that are occurring in the world demand that you embrace your Warrior, exert your power, acknowledge your value, and trust your truth, not in arrogance, but humbly accepting that you're on this planet for a purpose and you've been given everything you need to fulfill that purpose. Feel the force of your courage, the magnitude and glory of your Greatness, knowing you have touched the Divine and the Divine has big plans for you.

There may be a tendency to slip back into old ways. The familiar is seductive. But know you are closing this book a different person. If Greatness is what you truly desire, you're on the right path, pursuing your Soul's purpose for your own bliss and the benefit of others—and you *will be* richly rewarded. You may be required to take risks that feel uncomfortable, but now you know—discomfort is a sign of growth, the path to Greatness, a cause for celebration.

You cannot do this wrong. Receive everything that happens, from this moment forward, as a reason to rejoice in your triumphs, sort out your resistance, heal your past, or determine your next step.

Stay focused on the four stages to the best of your ability. They will lead you to more Greatness and Prosperity than you can even imagine at this point. Always remember to be patient and gentle with yourself. This is not about perfection. It's about persistence. *Sacred Success* is a journey without end, best taken in small steps.

Turn to *Sacred Success* graduate Tatiana Bredikin's words for inspiration: "When I am stuck, it only takes the smallest step in the direction of my dreams to get me moving again. Before I take it, I believe I will have to climb mountains and cross deserts to get back on track, but that's not true. The smallest action moves me."

As you travel the road to Greatness, commit this statement to memory, repeating it regularly: *Where I am, right now, is perfect. Where I go next depends on how much I'm willing to release and how much I'm willing to receive.*

Let your new mantra be: *I cannot, I will not, be less than I am for anyone! I AM going for Greatness and Prosperity with everything I've got!* Then expect miracles. They'll be there.

CHAPTER SUMMARY: Women Waking; Mountains Moving

- Something is happening in our world: Sleeping women are waking up, triggering a paradigm shift of major proportions.

- Unwilling to play by the old rules, women are writing new ones based on their cherished values and feminine traits.

- The so-called *women effect* is transforming the historical norm into what's becoming a clearly and increasingly preferred leadership style.

- As the feminine energy—which resides in both sexes (though often repressed in men)—is equally valued alongside the masculine, partnership is replacing polarization.

- The four stages of *Sacred Success* provide the transformational process necessary for navigating the new paradigm.

- The new paradigm demands that you embrace your Warrior, exert your power, acknowledge your value, trust your truth, and pursue your purpose, knowing you have everything you need to achieve Greatness.

- You may be required to take uncomfortable risks, but discomfort is a sign of growth, the path to Greatness, a cause for celebration.

- You cannot do this wrong. Everything that happens provides reason to rejoice in your triumphs, sort out your resistance, heal your past, or determine your next step.

- Be patient and gentle with yourself. *Sacred Success* is a journey without end, best taken in small steps.

- Remember this: Where you are, right now, is perfect. Where you go next depends on how much you're willing to release and how much you're willing to receive.

- Then watch for the miracles. They'll be there.

FINAL HOMEWORK

Your final assignments: Complete the Contract with Myself below. Then occasionally review this book, putting into practice what's been meaningful to you, sharing what you've learned with others.

Sacred Success® Action Plan: A Contract with Myself

Write a list of three to five action steps you are committing to take in the next thirty days. Then sign and date your contract and have a witness do the same. Every time you complete an action, cross it off and add another.

I, _____, do hereby commit I will do one thing
(your name)
on this list every day, for the next thirty days, to achieve Greatness.

1. _____	16. _____
2. _____	17. _____
3. _____	18. _____
4. _____	19. _____
5. _____	20. _____
6. _____	21. _____
7. _____	22. _____
8. _____	23. _____
9. _____	24. _____
10. _____	25. _____
11. _____	26. _____
12. _____	27. _____
13. _____	28. _____
14. _____	29. _____
15. _____	30. _____

_____

(your signature)   (date)

_____

(witness)   (date)

SACRED SUCCESS® SUGGESTED ACTION STEPS

Here are some examples of actions you can include in your contract. This is by no means a definitive list. Most are actions we discussed in the book. I offer them as ideas in case you draw a blank when filling out your contract.

- Refine my purpose.
- Meditate, sit in stillness, take time for solitude.
- Write in my Receiving Journal.
- Acknowledge and fully receive compliments.
- See "negative" experiences as a gift of useful information.
- Distinguish who is talking in my head: my Soul or my Ego.
- Find a financial advisor by asking people for names.
- Make an appointment to interview at least three potential advisors.
- Check in with my financial advisor.
- Ask friends: "What do you see in me that I don't see in myself?"
- Stretch by doing what I fear or do NOT want to do.
- Monitor and stop telling my old "story."
- Track my expenses. Put them in categories (see worksheets in appendix).
- Figure out my net worth (see worksheet in appendix).
- Create a *Sacred Success* Affirmation.
- Give myself a pep talk (or ask someone else to).
- Put my needs first ("I'd rather be respected than liked").
- Observe my self-depreciation; switch to self-praise instead.
- Write down the legacy I wish to leave.
- Pamper myself.
- Do something fun.
- Find time to relax.
- Ask myself: What do I *really* want?
- Reread parts of this book.
- Ask myself: Where am I out of integrity?

- Make sure I'm owning my value by sharing a "brag" with a friend.
- When unhappy, ask myself: Where am I giving my power away?
- Find at least one person to add to my love nest.
- Evaluate my profit and loss statement; make necessary changes.
- Find a mentor.
- Run a problem by a few members of my strategic team.
- No strategic team? Create one—ask people I admire to be sounding boards.
- Talk with my spouse/partner about our finances.
- Set up automatic deposit into my savings account.
- Talk to my Powerful Self.
- Figure out where I want to donate money, how much, by when.
- Read something about money.
- Contribute to retirement plan and/or private investments.

Appendix

Financial Documents

Expense Tracker

Make copies of the chart below. Carry them with you. Every time you make a purchase, write down the item, the amount you paid, and whether you're using cash, credit card, check, or debit card. It's too easy to fritter away money without knowing where it's gone. This exercise can be a real eye-opener.

Item	Amount	Form of Payment

The Monthly Money Flow Chart Summary

Make twelve copies of this chart so you have a year's worth. Every month, transfer your expenses from the Expense Tracker to the Monthly Money Flow Chart, putting your expenses into their relevant categories. Once you add up the totals in each category, transfer the totals to the Condensed Monthly Money Flow Chart (p. 218).

	Full Month Amount	Notes
Income		
Self		
Partner		
Other		
Total Income	$	
Savings/Investments		
Automatic Savings		
Money Market/CD Savings Accounts		
Retirement Accounts		
Stocks/Mutual Funds		
Total Savings/Investments	$	
Debt Payments		
Home Equity Line		
Education Loans		
Consumer/Auto Loans		
Total Credit Card Payments		
Other		
Total Debt Payments	$	
Household		
Supplies		
Furniture/Decorating		

(Continued)

	Full Month Amount	Notes
Landscape		
Repairs/Improvements		
Other		
Total Household	$	
Food		
Groceries		
Restaurants		
Other		
Total Food	$	
Clothing		
Wardrobe		
Accessories		
Cleaning		
Other		
Total Clothing	$	
Self-Care		
Supplies		
Health Club		
Services		
Cosmetics		
Other		
Total Self-Care	$	
Health Care		
Insurance		
Health Care Providers		
Supplements/Supplies		
Other		
Total Health Care	$	

(Continued)

	Full Month Amount	Notes
Transportation		
Car Payments/Rental/Public Transportation		
Insurance		
Registration		
Gas		
Repairs/Maintenance		
Other		
Total Transportation	$	
Entertainment		
Gatherings/Parties		
Movies/Video Rental		
Concerts/Theater, Etc.		
Sporting Events		
Subscriptions		
Vacations/Travel		
Other		
Total Entertainment	$	
Dependent Care		
Childcare		
Education		
Toys/Books/Supplies		
Medical		
Other Child Related		
Elderly Care		
Pet Food & Supplies		
Vet/Grooming		
Other Pet Related		
Total Dependent Care	$	

(Continued)

	Full Month Amount	Notes
Education		
Tuition		
Books		
Classes/Seminars		
Other		
Total Education	$	
Taxes & Insurance		
Federal Income Tax		
State Income Tax		
Life Insurance		
Homeowner's Insurance		
Other		
Total Taxes & Insurance	$	
Gifts		
Birthday		
Holiday/Special Occasion		
Other		
Total Gifts	$	
Spiritual Growth		
Church/Temple		
Education		
Total Spiritual Growth	$	

The Condensed Monthly Money Flow Chart Summary

By condensing the expense categories above, you get a bird's-eye view of your total spending. If you have money left over, congratulations! Use it to pay down credit card debt and add to savings. If the result is negative, go back to the Monthly Money Flow Chart and see where you can cut expenses. In addition, use this chart to see if you're spending in a way that reflects your values, goals, and dreams.

	Full Month Amount	Notes
Total Income	$	
Expenses		
Savings/Investments	$	
Debt Payments	$	
Household	$	
Food	$	
Clothing	$	
Self-Care	$	
Health Care	$	
Transportation	$	
Entertainment	$	
Dependent Care	$	
Education	$	
Taxes & Insurance	$	
Gifts	$	
Spiritual Growth	$	
Total Expenses	**$**	
Net Money Flow Subtract total expenses from total income	$	

Net Worth Calculation

Assets

Cash (or Equivalents)

Cash in Checking & Savings Accts. $ _____

Money Market Funds $ _____

Cash Value of Life Insurance $ _____

Loans Receivable $ _____

Other $ _____

Investments (Market Value)

Certificates of Deposit $ _____

Stocks $ _____

Bonds $ _____

Mutual Funds $ _____

Annuities $ _____

Retirement Funds

IRAs $ _____

401(k), 403(b), 457 Plans $ _____

Pension/Profit-Sharing Plan $ _____

Other $ _____

Real Estate (Current Market Value)

Residence $ _____

Income Property $ _____

Land $ _____

Self-Empl. Business Valuation (Net) $ _____

Personal Property

Automobile(s) $ _____

Recreational Vehicle/Boat $ _____

Household Furnishings $ _____

Collections/Art $ _____

Jewelry $ _____

Other $ _____

TOTAL ASSETS $ _____

Liabilities

Current Debts

Credit Cards $ _____

Department Store Cards $ _____

Medical $ _____

Back Taxes $ _____

Legal $ _____

Other $ _____

Loans

Personal (Bank/Finance Companies) $ _____

Home Equity $ _____

Education $ _____

Automobile $ _____

Recreational Vehicle/Boat $ _____

Education $ _____

Personal (from Friends/Family) $ _____

Other $ _____

Mortgages

Home(s) $ _____

Investment Properties $ _____

Land $ _____

Other $ _____

TOTAL LIABILITIES $ _____

Net Worth Calculation

Total Assets $ _____

Minus Total Liabilities $ _____

EQUALS NET WORTH $ _____

Vital Financial Information

Your Name: _____

Social Security Number: _____

Key People to Contact (name, phone number, etc.)

Attorney: _____

Accountant: _____

Financial Advisor: _____

Other: _____

Location of Vital Documents

Will: _____

Tax Returns: _____

Insurance Papers: _____

Deed to House: _____

Mortgage: _____

Other: _____

Insurance Policies, Account Numbers, and Contact People: _____

_____

Banks and/or Institutions, Account Numbers, and Contact People: _____

_____

Retirement Account, Account Numbers, and Contact People: _____

_____

Location of Safety Deposit Box and Key: _____

_____

Credit Cards: _____

_____

_____

_____

Index

About the Author

Photo by Frank Ross

Barbara Stanny, the leading authority on women and money, is a bestselling author, teacher, and wealth coach. Barbara has helped millions take charge of their finances and their lives.

Barbara's background in business and career development, her master's degree in counseling psychology, her extensive research, and her own dramatic story with money give her a unique and powerful perspective on women's financial issues.

Barbara is the author of five other books:

- *Prince Charming Isn't Coming: How Women Get Smart About Money*
- *Secrets of Six-Figure Women*
- *Overcoming Underearning*
- *Finding a Financial Advisor You Can Trust*
- *Breaking Through: Getting Past the Stuck Points in Your Life*

Barbara and her husband live in a log cabin in Port Townsend, Washington. Visit her at www.barbarastanny.com.